Information 2000

INSIGHTS INTO THE COMING DECADES IN INFORMATION
TECHNOLOGY

Information 2000

INSIGHTS INTO
THE COMING DECADES
IN INFORMATION
TECHNOLOGY

Edited by David Clutterbuck

PITMAN PUBLISHING
128 Long Acre, London WC2E 9AN

A Division of Longman Group UK Limited

© The BIS Group Limited 1989

First published 1989

British Library Cataloguing in Publication Data

Clutterbuck, David, 1947–
    Information 2000 insights into the coming decades in information technology.
    1. Great Britain. Business firms. Management.
    Information systems. Applications of computer systems
    I. Title
    658.4'038

ISBN 0 273 03093 0

Typesetting by Wyvern Typesetting Ltd, Bristol

Printed and bound in Great Britain
at The Bath Press, Avon

CONTENTS

FOREWORD

by The Prime Minister, The Right Honourable Margaret Thatcher

I am very pleased to have this opportunity to congratulate the BIS Group on its Silver Jubilee.

Industry and commerce have changed greatly during the past twenty-five years, but nowhere have the changes been· more marked than in the Information Technology sector.

Not only has the technology advanced almost beyond all recognition, but information technology now pervades almost every other sector of modern business. The success of the BIS Group and similar companies now contributes enormously to the competitiveness of many British companies.

During its twenty-five years BIS has grown to nearly 2000 people and has a multimillion pound turnover, about half of which is earned overseas.

As this collection of essays shows, enormous changes will continue, and I wish BIS and its clients every success in tackling the opportunities and challenges that will arise in the coming years.

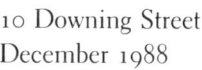

10 Downing Street
December 1988

INTRODUCTION

The contributors to this collection of essays are fortunate in being involved in an industry that embraces computing and marketing services. Few other business sectors have experienced such tremendous and consistent growth and change since the 1960s as has information technology. While the occasion for the publishing of this volume is the twenty-fifth anniversary of the founding of the BIS Group in 1964, its purpose is not to look back. The chapters, mainly written by colleagues in the BIS Group and its parent NYNEX Corporation, are principally concerned with looking forward to the future role of information in society in the coming decades.

The working environment affects both how people approach their day-to-day activities and how they view the future. Readers of these articles will find a considerable optimism about the role of information and technologies affecting it. Much of this is founded in the basic beliefs that have guided the BIS Group from its infancy to its current position as a leader in its various fields with some two thousand people worldwide.

Brian Allison, the founder of the Group and its chairman until September 1987, had the far-sightedness from the start to see the connections between marketing, computing and training. Service organisations promoting new ideas and delivering change are particularly dependent on people. Our principal assets are our customers and our staff. We seek long-term relationships with customers by assisting them to achieve profitable growth and increased productivity. BIS people make this happen, by providing innovative solutions based on quality products and services. Organisationally, we believe in a decentralised approach that gives responsibility to some one hundred management teams across the Group. These teams typically include both general business managers and specialists.

Increasingly our businesses share common customers, and rely on people with similar skills to bring benefits from creativity and technology. This community of interest across the Group provides a framework for our future development and the background against which these essays are written.

In the opening chapter, which provides a broad overview of the whole terrain of information, Roger Graham places information technology in an historical context and looks at its emergence as a major force in the business world. He considers the shift in employment patterns over the long term; the importance of information in the global economy; and the ever-rising demand for information products and services.

Brian Allison discusses the challenges of managing with information–the use of information at the highest level of business, in the boardroom. He analyses the need for information within large organisations; how attitudes to information management have changed in recent years; and the strategic possibilities being opened up by new technology.

Garf Collins explores the use of computer systems to deliver information to users. He explains the concern of senior managers about both the effectiveness and the efficiency of their systems. He also proposes ways in which people who depend upon information for their survival can ensure they receive the information they need accurately, at the right time and in a readily usable form.

Mike Gordon describes how the electronics industry – that provides equipment on which the information society is based – is structured and predicts how it will develop. He argues firstly, that this is one field in which big is undeniably beautiful; and secondly, that Europe has to face up to the challenge of restructuring for rapid growth, if it intends to continue to compete in the world market.

Gad Selig foresees a trillion dollar tomorrow for the information industry. He maps out how the various subsectors of the industry may evolve, highlighting a number of key business management issues, which the primary contestants will need to face. In this article he is assisted by Harvey Poppel of Broadview Associates, a leading US consultancy which specialises in acquisitions and mergers and is an advisor to the BIS Group.

Cas Skrzypczak examines how computers and telecommunications are slowly but surely converging. He gives a tantalising glimpse of when this convergence will make many new products and services available.

The following four chapters deal with some significant new applications of information technology to business services: in financial services, in marketing, in economic forecasting and in the printing and publishing world. These are four types of business service all rooted in computing methods, which have grown up in the past 25 years and in which the BIS Group has special expertise.

Rob Wood investigates the financial services revolution. He shows why banks and insurance and investment companies have been among the leaders in pioneering information technology and looks at the intensifying competition between the top organisations.

Alan Bigg traces the rise of direct marketing as a challenge to advertising. He contends that the development of the computer database gives its owner a competitive edge as a potentially far more effective means of communicating with customers.

Frank Gelber assesses the claims of economic forecasters that they make a significant contribution to business management. He suggests that the technology base of forecasting will not advance significantly in the next decade, but that managers can use forecasts more effectively, if they understand the basis on which they are made.

Rai Wasner depicts the revolution going on in the world of electronic imaging – copiers, faxes, printers, desktop publishing systems and the like. He believes the quality of presentation will become a strategic weapon in information processing.

Garf Collins gives us a vision of our homes in the future. He advises that the development of our electronic cottage will not be simple or smooth but rather a result of the coming together of the four major applications clusters.

In a postcript, Richard Pearson of the Institute of Management Studies emphasises that the whole information industry is a people business and that the chief restriction to growth is the shortage of trained people. He chronicles the crisis in skills shortage and suggests some ways in which it can be alleviated.

No book on such a huge subject can claim to be comprehensive. However, in *Information 2000* we have provided an overview of this fascinating industry from the privileged viewpoint of a group of acknowledged authorities – writers whose authority rests on their rich experience of the past twenty-five years.

ACKNOWLEDGEMENTS

The BIS Group would like to thank the many people involved in the production of this book. First, I very much appreciate the way in which the Rt Hon Margaret Thatcher has contributed a foreword to this volume.

The authors are not only experts in the field of Information Technology but busy businessmen and I appreciate the time and effort they have devoted to this project. Co-ordinating the work of many contributors demands considerable editorial skill and we thank Mr David Clutterbuck for the work he has done as editor in bringing the book together. Also, Mr George Black played an important role in the early conception of the book and was responsible for the initial editorial work.

Finally, I would like to express our appreciation for the work of Mrs Sandra Verity who assumed responsibility for overseeing the prodcution of the book in the final, critical stages and who has been invaluable in the work leading to the successful launch of the book.

ROGER GRAHAM OBE
Chairman & Managing Director
BIS Group   March 1989

CONTRIBUTORS

Brian Allison, Founder and former Executive Chairman, BIS Group
Alan Bigg, Chairman, Christian Brann Ltd
David Clutterbuck (Editor), Chairman ITEM Group
Garfield Collins, Managing Director, BIS Applied Systems
Frank Gelber, Director of Economic and Building Services, BIS Shrapnel
Michael Gordon, Managing Director, BIS Mackintosh
Roger Graham OBE, Chairman and Managing Director, BIS Group
Richard Pearson, Deputy Director, Institute of Manpower Studies
Harvey Poppel, Partner, Broadview Associates
Dr. Gad J. Selig, Vice President of Marketing and Technology and
    Business Development, NYNEX Information Solutions Group
Casimir Skrzypczak, Vice President, Science and Technology, NYNEX
    Corporation
Raimund Wasner, Senior Vice President, CAP International
Robin Wood, Marketing and Planning Manager, BIS Group

1

INFORMATION 2000: A PROLOGUE

'Many technologies have had significant impacts on people's lives during the twentieth century, but none so profound as information technology (IT). Yet the benefits of IT are still only beginning to be seen. As we approach the next century, systems which are easier to use and more flexible will bring IT into many more applications at work and in the home. These developments will pose major challenges both for software developers and for IT users' says Roger Graham, Chairman and Managing Director of the BIS Group.

When the world was young, men depicted the stories of their lives on the walls of caves; later came the printed word; now electronics has arrived to record and communicate both our doings and our expectations.

The past hundred years have seen technology in its many forms have an unparalleled effect on our lives. It has been the principal contributor to increasing the real standard of living of people in the industrialised world five-fold. Advances in medicine have nearly doubled life expectancy from just over forty years to the mid-seventies in those countries and together with other technologies have greatly enhanced the quality of life for those who would otherwise have been disabled. Largely as a result of technology, the hours spent in paid employment have nearly halved, while the years spent in full-time education have nearly doubled. Supported by basic discoveries in physics and chemistry, almost all fields of technology have made contributions to the massive increases in the underlying productivity of people at work, in passage or at home (see Table 1.1).

Table 1.1 Paid employment as a percentage of awake lifetime

Year	%
1880	42
1945	28
1985	18
2000	14–16

THE UNIQUENESS OF INFORMATION TECHNOLOGY

The pace of change has quickened since the 1950s with the application of a new set of technologies related to the processing and communication of information. Throughout the centuries major advances in society have been greatly affected by improvements in information handling and dissemination. However, information technology, which embraces computing and telecommunications, is exceptional. No previous technology has advanced at such a pace. Year-on-year the price performance of the underlying computer technology has improved 20–30 per cent. The personal computer I have on my desk has 100 times more power and storage and costs just 1 per cent of the price of the first commercial computer I installed 25 years ago.

We have moved a long way since the pioneering days in the 1950s, when the experts thought that just a few computers would meet the needs of society and that those would only be used by governments and major organisations. They believed that the role of computers would be primarily for complex mathematical analysis. But it rapidly became clear that many large organisations could take advantage of the computer's ability to improve the timeliness, accuracy and content of information flows, both within the business and with customers and suppliers.

Today our expectations from computing and associated telecommunications know few boundaries. These technologies are not simply applied to keeping track of past events but are increasingly used as tools to win customers, provide more flexible manufacturing systems, deliver quality service and determine the future. Computers linked together by networked telecommunications are ever more pervasive in the workplace, in the high street and at home. No longer do increases in productivity depend on treating people in the same way as part of a mass market. Information technology has created the option to treat individuals according to their own wants and needs and to offer choice and diversity. An altogether more stimulating world of mass individualism is in prospect.

THE RISE OF THE SERVICE SECTOR

These changes have been accompanied by a widely recognised shift of economic activity from the goods-producing to the service sector. In the United States of America, 76 per cent of the workforce, 68 per cent of real GNP and 90 per cent of all new jobs arise from the service sector (including government). One of the myths of even recent years has been the extent of employment in the manufacturing sector–in the USA it was never more than 30 per cent.

Table 1.2 Service sector percentage of GDP and workforce

Country	% GDP	% Workforce
USA	68	76
West Germany	54	53
United Kingdom	56	63
Japan	58	55
Sweden	63	67

Certainly, there are fewer blue-collar jobs than there were, particularly in agriculture and mining. Yet in manufacturing companies the proportion of service occupations in, for instance, design, marketing and sales has been growing steadily since the turn of the century. The role of these 'knowledge workers' has become increasingly important as success in manufacturing becomes more and more based on information or software. Designing, producing and delivering quality, competitively advantaged products depends increasingly on effective information systems. As product life cycles shorten and optional features are incorporated to meet individual market preferences, information becomes a prerequisite to production.

The growth of information technology in the workplace relies as much on the strength and growth of service occupations as on its application in the goods manufacturing sector. Many of the humdrum, blue-collar occupations being displaced by computer-based, flexible manufacturing are being replaced by jobs in growing service activities.

The newer service occupations are less vulnerable to boom-and-bust cycles than manufacturing has been. One reason is the absence of an inventory cycle in the service sector. Another is that many of the occupations themsleves are more transferable between industries than are traditional manufacturing skills. Furthermore, the service sector has continued to generate jobs in periods of recession and those jobs are often increasingly well paid and capitally intensive.

For example, our company the BIS Group, a worldwide computer and marketing services organisation employing some 2000 people, has doubled the value of capital equipment supporting each staff member to nearly $20 000 in the past five years. Some service sector jobs, for example in transportation and energy production, have always been dependent on massive fixed assets. Only in recent years have information-based jobs in, for instance, finance, law, marketing and even education, medicine and government become similarly reliant on fixed assets–this time in the form of information equipment in the workplace. Much of this equipment consists of computer-based workstations and includes copiers, facsimile machines and digitial communications. Before the year 2000, 80 per cent of people in such occupations will have the personal use of intelligent computer-based workstations.

While the physical manifestation of information technology appears in equipment of many types, its value is increasingly determined by the software, which gives the basic devices their capability to be useful. People buy television sets for the programmes they can view, not simply to have a rectangle of dark glass in the corner of their living rooms. The TV programme or software is the essence of the value that people put upon the system.

THE GROWTH OF THE COMPUTER SERVICES SECTOR

It takes many supporting services to provide the software and make it useable by non-specialists. As a consequence, a whole new information services industry has developed, employing some one million people around the globe. Additionally some 2.5 million people are engaged as specialists in organisations using computer-based information systems. The role of all these people is to help make the changes that allow computer-based information to contribute effectively to the organisation's goals. By the end of the century there will be some 6–8 million of these specialists.

Because it enhances the technology of the hardware, the computing services industry, which is concerned with the provision, application and operation of software, has seen its own spectacular year-on-year growth. Indeed, the growth rate in software has been double that of hardware and this will continue through to the end of the century, although the sizes of the hardware and software business are now similar.

The computer services sector is now being seen in the context of a wider information services industry embracing information transport (telecommunications and post) and information content (publishing, marketing and advertising service)–see Table 1.3.

Table 1.3 *The US information services industry*

	US 1990: $ bill	Growth rate 1982–90 (%)
Information management		
Computing services	78	20
Information transport	162	9
Local telecommunications	45	
Long distance telecommunications	71	
Post	46	
Information content		
Publishing	92	6
Marketing services and printing	56	6–17
Entertainment (software and broadcasting)	99	9

(*Source:* Booz, Allen & Hamiltion)

The convergence of these sectors and some other industries highly dependent on information—such as banking, insurance, professional accounting services and even hi-technology manufacturing—will increase. Leading companies in these sectors will seek a major stake in the information services industry, particularly as they recognise the opportunity to differentiate their base business by the quality of their use of information. Reuters, basically a publisher and until the mid-seventies a worldwide news agency, has transformed its business with its success in providing networked financial information through some 100 000 screeens around the globe. General Motors and McDonnell-Douglas have not only invested hugely in information systems to support the design, production and distribution of their own products, but have also acquired specialist computer service companies. Citicorp and National Westminster Bank both provide computing services and software to their clients and users. Dunn and Bradstreet, originally a vendor of credit information, has diversified into a marketing database supplier, whose operations are based on computers. Likewise, the major professional accounting practices have established substantial management consulting operations with particular emphasis on computer application. (Figure 1.1)

Large organisations in these sectors will seek a substantial stake in the electronic and software-based information services industry. Wherever business is complex, rapidly changing or highly competitive, the quality of information systems and particularly the software that drives them will be the principal determinant of continuing success. Organisations that seek or need to operate in many locations (whether domestic or international) will rely on networked information systems. Timely, relevant information that enhances

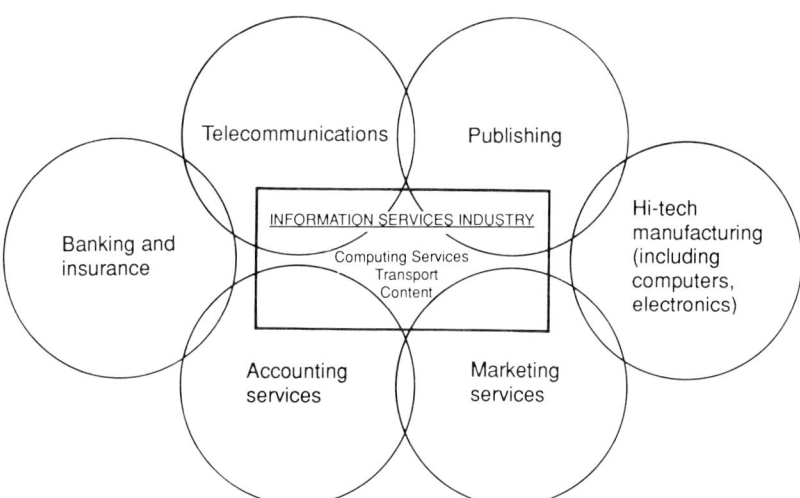

Figure 1.1   Information services industry convergence

understanding, facilitates decisions and enables early action will be *the* competitive advantage. The idea is not new. Rothschild made a fortune by using a carrier pigeon to convey the news of the outcome of the Battle of Waterloo and so anticipated the response of the London financial markets. The difference today is that the technology is universally available.

THE LIMITATIONS OF INFORMATION TECHNOLOGY TODAY

Nonetheless, the gulf between the potential of IT and current realities is vast. Executives are concerned that the new information systems often fail to meet expectations. Too often systems cost more than has been budgeted, are late in delivery and inflexible in use. While systems that provide high volume transaction processing of routine tasks are generally satisfactory, analytical and decision support systems now pose more challenging problems.

The lengthy procedures and large teams of people required make many IT development projects difficult to justify. Even when the benefits are clearly worth the investment, the resultant systems can be unresponsive to changed business circumstances. The quality and security of systems become more of a concern as business and government rely on computers and communications for basic operations and for critical defence and transportation applications. Part of the solution is to educate and train non-specialists to deal with the new

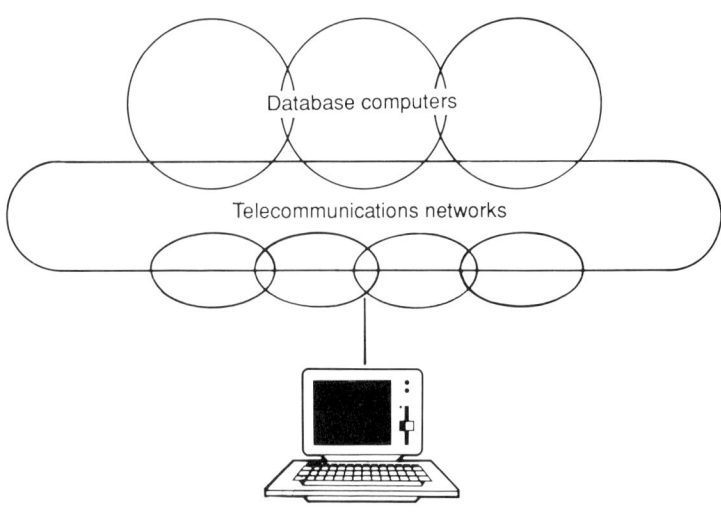

Figure 1.2   Systems connectivity

technology. But this can only happen when systems become altogether easier to use.

Ease of use in turn depends on software that enables systems that operate on different computing equipment and with different software to communicate and be connected to one another – see Figure 1.2.

THE FUTURE WITH INFORMATION TECHNOLOGY

The major opportunity for the software industry is systems integration, which involves the connection of massive databases, telecommunications network links and personal workstations. For the user, it will involve workstations, similar to the telephone, which have broad access to millions of others and are connectable to an enormous diversity of information data-banks. These workstations will communicate with users not only with text, numbers and simple graphics but also with speech, full colour images and video. They, in turn, will be responsive to voice, and to touch (not just keyboards but also on screen and through handwriting on simple pads). Paper will still be an important medium and workstations will all have access to local, compact hybrid devices that can print, copy, send and receive facsimile. The user himself will increasingly decide how he uses these facilities; he will be much less constrained by systems and operating procedures prescribed by specialists. While complex systems for managing applications in, for instance, finance, transportation, or defence, will continue to require precise definition, they will be more adaptable to changing requirements and to supporting unstructured activities.

The role of the software industry is to make these capabilities available. It is maturing from an industry dominated by technical specialists to one that understands the needs of users, has the experience to manage large complex projects and possesses the tools and professionalism to deliver the promise. It will extend its expertise beyond conventional data processing and become more involved with image, video and audio systems as well as telecommunications software. It will use computer-based tools for the development of new software, which will be more reliable and enhanceable. It will not only build and deliver new systems, but will also operate facilities for users on a continuing basis. It will enable companies to build competitive advantage through knowledge data bases and dynamic market and operational information.

Progress will depend not just on software people but also on users. Unless top management can provide a clear vision of the role, which information can play in promoting competitive advantage, the benefits of advancing technologies will be left to competitors—see Table 1.4.

Table 1.4 *Use of IT administration and strategy*

	5 years ago (%)	Now (%)	5 years time (%)
Internal administration	46	65	73
Operational strategies	13	35	57
Broad Ratio: strategic/administration use	1/4	1/2	3/4

(*Source: Financial Times*)

While managers have never needed to know how to program a computer, they do need to understand the capabilities of information systems. They have to know what IT can do for their operations, what new facilities will soon be available, what competitors are doing. They need to turn this knowledge to practical advantage by involving all levels of the organisation in determining both prospective benefits and how to seize them. Above all, they must learn to enjoy change and have the ability to lead others to enjoy it as well.

The effects of the new information technology will not only be felt in the workplace. Electronics in the home has had the highest growth rate of all consumer expenditures in recent years—see Table 1.5.

Table 1.5 *Consumer expenditure (constant 1980 prices)*

	1978	1980	1985
Books, newspapers	97	100	93
Food	98	100	102
Energy	99	100	103
Housing	95	100	110
Household durable goods	94	100	118
Vehicles	93	100	126
TVs, videos, PCs, etc	90	100	167

While the cost of most other items has increased, electronic information equipment has consistently declined in cost as its functionality increased. Until now, much of the equipment has been for the one-way receiving of information. Even home computers have been largely applied for entertainment purposes. People spend on average 4–5 hours a day watching television, the most time-consuming leisure activity. The lifestyles that people live at home do not rely on the structured information systems that people expect at work. However, the linkage of television and home computer screens to telecommunications networks including cable and satellite television systems provide new possibilities—see Table 1.6.

Progress with interactive home information systems is likely to be slow. It will start with those who transfer some of their paid employment activity to home. Home working by information workers will grow for a number of reasons, among them lifestyle trends involving more part-time work, non-traditional career paths requiring retraining, e.g. qualified lawyers moving into business/

Table 1.6 Consumer demand for application of new technology

	0%	10%	20%	30%	40%
Banking/bills	XXXXXXXXXXXXXXXXXXX 40 XXXXXXXXXXXXXXXXXXX				
Entertainment/tickets	XXXXXXXXXXXXXXXXX 36 XXXXXXXXXXXXXXXXX				
Household budget	XXXXXXXXXXXXXXXX 34 XXXXXXXXXXXXXXXX				
Personal calendar	XXXXXXXXXXXXXXX 32 XXXXXXXXXXXXXXX				
Energy and security	XXXXXXXXXXXXX 28 XXXXXXXXXXXXX				
Vocation/travel	XXXXXXXXXX 21 XXXXXXXXXX				
Learning	XXXXXXXXX 20 XXXXXXXXX				
Games	XXXXXXXXX 19 XXXXXXXX				
News	XXXXXXX 16 XXXXXXX				
Shopping	XXXXXXX 16 XXXXXXX				
Electronic mail	XXXXX 11 XXXXX				
Classified ads	XXXXX 11 XXXXX				
Insurance	XXXX 8 XXXX				
Investments	XXXX 7 XXX				

(*Source:* Booz, Allen & Hamilton)

management roles, graduates joining blue chip employers and moving on to a small company after a few years, more women in the work force, earlier retirement.

These new homeworkers will receive much of their training on their home computers. Familiarity with the equipment will encourage them to make more use of home computing and telecommunications to manage their finances and do home-shopping. Computers will monitor the home's environmental, energy and security management systems. Initially these applications will be used by a minority of the population, with home-shopping likely to be the first application that brings two-way computer-based information systems to the majority at home.

The need to communicate information was not born with the computer. It is as old as Man. The computer has given us the power to treat men and women as individuals with personal needs and wants. The experience of the era of mass production, media and communication with all its implications for boring standardisation are giving way to an information society providing mass individualism full of diversity and choice.

2

MANAGING WITH INFORMATION

'For today's chief executive, sorting out and obtaining information critical to the health of his business is one of the most perplexing tasks. It is not that there is inadequate information, but that there is too much background noise for him to tune in to the stations he needs. The solution', says Brian Allison, founder and former Executive Chairman of the BIS Group, 'lies in careful planning and design of reporting systems that are focused closely on the real business information needs.'

There is no royal road to effectively managing with information. The individual style and needs of organisations greatly affect the management principles by which they are run, their information needs and their information gathering systems. For example, as a company becomes more mature, larger, more diverse, more geographically widespread and nowadays probably more decentralised, its information system needs to be more and more rigorous and yet also increasingly filtered if it is to maintain proper control. As soon as the company starts to move from a single profit centre to two or more profit centres, the need for information systems and information flow increases sharply. The process is much like the development of aeroplanes. The very earliest aircraft, such as the Tiger Moth, were flown with very few instruments, 'by the seat of the pants', as they said. The pilot could look over the side and find out where he was going. He did almost everything visually and by quick reaction.

As aircraft became more complicated, through twin-engine executive machines to medium-size airliners such as the Boeing 737 up to the 'Jumbo' Boeing 747, the information systems, especially for early warning, needed to be more and more complex. They had to cope with environments which were ever more demanding. In today's aircraft the pilot is, in the main, a monitor of information systems and the final backstop in the event of an emergency.

So it is in business. A quarter of a century ago, management information systems were quite rudimentary, simplistic, not well developed and not well understood. They were rarely, if ever, driven by sophisticated computer technology. Most systems were then based on transaction processing and accounting needs and produced mainly historical information. They offered little operational data, particularly on markets, people or production and were of limited use in terms of forecasting, developing strategy, and new products and services.

THE CEO'S DILEMMA

Over the past 25 years we have seen a great improvement in the systems, which are available.

The big difficulty for managers today is not how to process information but how to decide what information they need to run their businesses effectively– what they need hourly, daily, weekly, monthly, quarterly and yearly. It is the challenge of selectivity and understanding; whereas the problem used to be that of too little information, it is now that of too much information. Today many managers are suffering from a great overdose of printed information, output from computers and so on. The question therefore is, how can we make the reporting system simple and manageable but effective?

In February 1984, the magazine *Chief Executive* published the results of a survey of 237 managing directors. They were asked to comment on the proposition that business was suffering from a surfeit of data, a 'data bombardment', but at the same time still had a scarcity of properly processed and useable information. Some 70 per cent agreed with this proposition. One of the main findings of the survey was that managing directors spend much more time reading and acting on information than they did only a few years earlier. Figure 2.1 shows that a high proportion of managing directors are

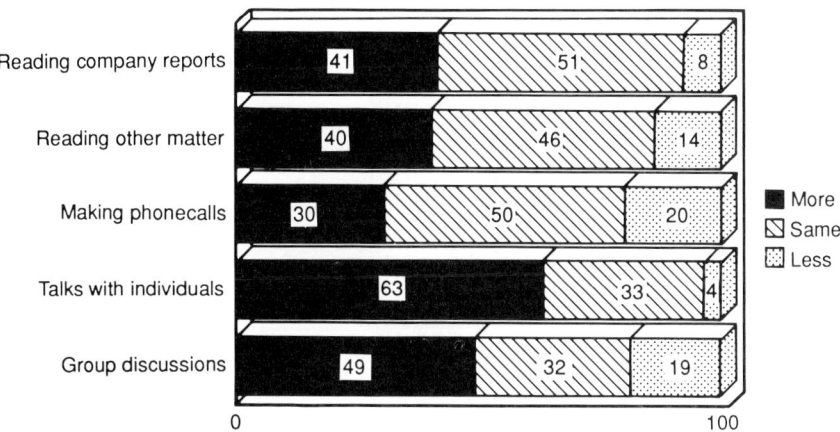

Figure 2.1   Percentages of MDs now spending more, the same or less time on different forms of information gathering (*Source: Chief Executive, February 1984. Reproduced by permission of Morgan-Grampian plc*)

reading more company reports and other material relating to businesses and markets. In particular, they are talking to many more people.

This is a healthy trend, but it does present key managers with many more difficult choices.

Figure 2.2 shows the frequency with which managing directors are getting reports, written or oral, on key facets of their business. A high percentage were getting at least weekly reports on sales, production and cash, and at least monthly on stock, debtors and (most encouraging) on market conditions and staff, a great change from a decade ago.

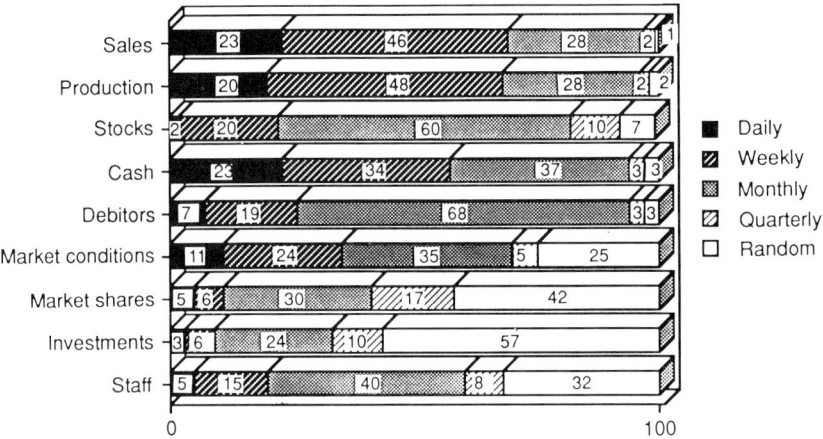

Figure 2.2   Percentages of MDs receiving reports on specific subjects at frequencies ranging from daily to random (*Source: Chief Executive, February 1984. Reproduced by permission of Morgan-Grampian plc*)

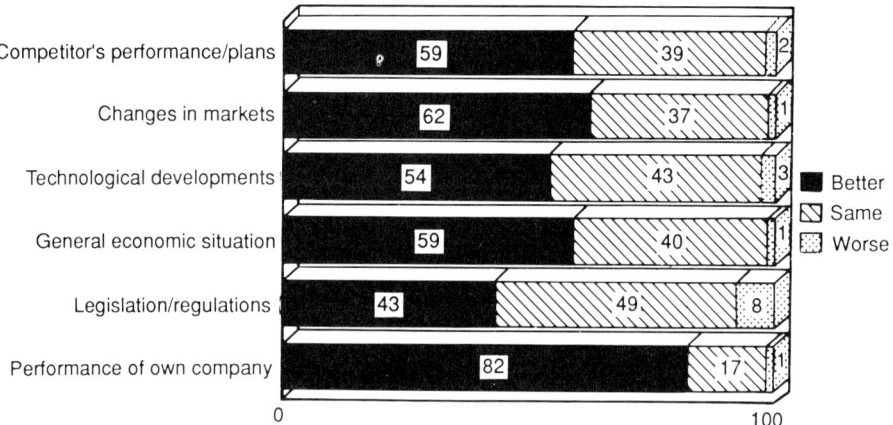

Figure 2.3   Percentage of MDs considering themselves better, the same or worse informed on various subjects than five years ago (*Source: Chief Executive, February 1984. Reproduced by permission of Morgan-Grampian plc*)

Despite any misgivings about data bombardment, just over half of the managing directors considered themselves to be better informed than they had been five years previously. Figure 2.3 shows one particular area—external factors affecting their companies' performance. For example, they feel more aware of changes in their markets and in competitive position, of technological developments and of the general economic situation.

PLANNING AS THE FOCUS FOR MANAGING INFORMATION

The main problems for today's top executives seem to be the sheer weight of information they receive and their ability to handle it so that they can take appropriate action. The well known official receiver Sir Kenneth Cork once explained that, in most bankrupt companies he had dealt with, top management could not answer basic questions about performance. When he demanded information, he would be given a 12 inch thick pile of computer print-outs and told 'I know it's in here somewhere, if we can work it out'. Top management needs information, which is timely, relevant and easy to understand. How, then, can a manager obtain the necessary reports to control his business effectively?

The starting point must be planning. A corporate plan should encompass the vision of where the company is going, its strategy and tactics. Without such a basis no company can function to its optimum. The plan should be a statement of realistic ambitions and should specify financial targets for both existing and new businesses. It should analyse the gaps, which are shown up; identify in outline new projects to fill those gaps; cover the logistics (people, money, premises, equipment, and so on) needed to fulfill the ambition; and give an account of the risks and contingencies involved.

The output of this planning process provides the basis for monitoring the progress of the company through a reporting system.

THE PRINCIPLES OF REPORTING

The general principle of a good reporting system is that it should be based on the concept of 'responsibility with authority'. The trouble with so much of British industry and commerce is that managers are given a lot of responsibility but not much authority.

In that environment, reporting systems may become meaningless. Without adequate authority senior managers' efforts are often diverted to concealing information and to indulging in self-protection. Further down the line, if people do not believe that the information they are giving is necessary and valuable, they will not take the trouble to ensure the information they are giving is reliable, so they corrupt the reporting system. The objective of any such system should be to create 'the owner's eye', rather than 'the employee's eye', in the person reporting. Any reporting system must be self-policing and not suffocating. If the information produced is not of value to the person reporting, it is unlikely to be of value to the person receiving it.

Reporting should also be forward-looking, so that it provides an early warning system – too many companies still have backward-looking reporting systems based upon historical information. Going back to our aircraft analogy, a reporting system is like the weather radar which can warn you that thunder clouds are coming up. The system must operate to ensure there are no surprises, no unexpected thunderstorms. A bad reporting system, typical in many bureaucracies, is one in which a lot of information is collected unnecessarily. Because it becomes a meaningless chore, no one takes any notice of the warning signs of a real emergency, until it is on top of them.

In sum, reporting systems must encourage a form of self-management, of business good housekeeping and stocktaking, whereby each month a manager reviews standard facets and key features of his business as if he were doing his own personal accounts. In doing so he almost automatically becomes much better informed. This attitude to management information should become part of the culture of the successful company.

THE BIS REPORTING SYSTEM

At the BIS Group we have developed our monthly reporting system carefully over the past 25 years. Our system begins with an account of the significant developments for each company and for each division within a company. These are the key events or achievements of the month being reported. This part of the report is designed to highlight for the unit manager or division manager and for top managers exactly what has been happening. It may cover, for example, exceptional profits or losses, major contracts won or lost, or significant marketing achievements. In essence, it is a summary of operating highlights.

Next we describe our setbacks, problems and proposed solutions in a matter-of-fact, no blame manner – still, I think, a rare feature of a reporting system. Far too few companies insist on this kind of formal, continuous evaluation. As a result their managers are not encouraged to be frank, as they should be. We need to communicate to our managers that it is not a sin to admit mistakes or to admit to having problems; but what we do ask from them is proposed solutions to problems.

We try to eliminate surprises and to offer support to people in difficulties from everyone else in the management team. This means that managers can accept and learn from mistakes. After all, business is all about taking well-judged risks and it is one of the functions of management to accept and manage risk.

Our financial reports set out clearly actual revenue, sales, profits and losses compared to budgets and they indicate significant variances and the reasons for them. But, more importantly, they concentrate on future projected revenue, sales, profits and losses and cash flow. Updated balance sheets are included, with key movements and assets and liabilities highlighted. This is done for every main profit centre throughout the organisation.

From the various financial data collected, we assemble a whole range of management ratios for the organisation and for individual operating units. These include measures of productivity and growth, percentages of costs versus revenues, and so on. The aim is to provide an early warning system by monitoring the changes and trends, much like the instrument panel of an aircraft.

Similarly, we give information about major contracts won and on the backlog situation – that is, the volume of business won but not yet implemented or billed. This is a crucial measure and by looking at the percentage of backlog against the revenue target, we can see the extent to which the company is either exceeding or falling below its required rate of growth.

Top management also needs to know what promotional events are planned. We would be very suspicious if a unit had no promotional events for several months running, because promotional campaigns give an indication of the future level of marketing activity.

All companies have products and services which have life cycles. Almost all of them rise, mature and in the long run decline, unless action is taken to change, enhance or replace them. Thus it is important to ensure that the company regularly looks at new ventures. It is important also to report the current state of any statutory and legal matters and what steps are being taken to resolve them.

Finally we report on people-related matters; changes in the numbers of people by various categories, organisational changes and administrative subjects such as accommodation, pay and pensions.

Thus the BIS Group in a document of some 40 pages gains a complete perspective on the progress of its plan, its operational status and a mass of early warning indicators. This is backed up with similar reports on each of the main operating divisions. It is the responsibility of each of the divisions to produce its own report, which is done by individual heads, their senior managers and financial officers, and these divisional reports are then integrated into the Group's monthly progress report to the executive and main boards.

Particularly important in an organisation with many profit centres or operating units is a reporting system which helps in the job of co-ordination, making sure that the units fit in with the strategy of the whole business. It must be possible to compare the performance of one unit with another and to assess the real contribution to the bottom line of each unit.

A good reporting system makes for discipline, makes leadership easier and helps to avoid crises, whether they be cash shortage, low sales, low backlog, errors in computer systems or problems with customers. It helps to bring clarity to the whole management process.

We can summarise the thinking behind the system, by which data is consistently collected at BIS Group, in a set of 'Twelve Commandments'. (Table 2.1).

Table 2.1　'The twelve commandments'

Finance
1　Consolidation–group needs
2　Cash–needs, availability, conservation
3　Comparison–versus plan/budget
4　Consistency–forecasting standards
5　Company law–legal/fiscal requirements

Operations
6　Communications–two-way
7　Co-ordination ⎫
8　Comparability ⎬ –of operating units
9　Contribution ⎭

Management attitudes
10　Culture–discipline and leadership
11　Crisis avoidance–early warning
12　Clarity–thought and logic

INFORMATION INTO ACTION

Nonetheless, it is no use having splendid reports of the sort outlined above if nobody reviews them thoroughly and regularly or does anything about them.

Communications within a company must be two-way. The board should not just receive reports; it has to follow them up by telling the middle managers what it feels about those reports and what is happening at the corporate level.

There is an information imbalance in many companies today. Their middle managers, in particular, seem to feel that they are being asked to give a great deal of information to their superiors without knowing why it is required or what is to be done with it. Often they get very little feedback.

Within BIS we have three levels of review and action on our reports:

- first, by the Group board, which meets quarterly;
- secondly, by the executive board, which meets monthly and consists of top management and the heads of the operating companies;
- and thirdly, by the operating companies themselves, which have their own boards or management group meeting monthly or less frequently.

INFORMATION FOR BOARD PURPOSES

The main purposes of board meetings, based on my thirty years' personal experience of business are set out below.

1 Boards have to ensure that companies and divisions meet the legal requirements of their society and to formally sanction the principal actions being taken within the company.

2 They have to take major policy decisions about strategy.

3 They have to review, understand and do something about any major problems.

4 Using the progress report they should regularly review operational progress.

5 They provide a forum for information exchange, involving the members of the board in matters which, though not their immediate responsibility, help their understanding and performance and co-ordinate their activities.

6 They should help in directors' own career development, through participation in decision-making.

7 They should encourage team-building, which is essential in a decentralised framework.

Information gathering and availability impinges on all these board purposes and processes.

INFORMATION TECHNOLOGY AND THE BOARDROOM

One of the problems with British industry over the past quarter-century has been, not that our managers are fools, but that they have not had the proper information on which to make crucial decisions. This failure stems partially from an inability to be more selective in our information needs, in order to reduce the paper mountain and partially from an inability to ask the right questions. The first of these require advanced technology which, to a significant extent, we now have.

One way in which technology is beginning to ease the problem of the data bombardment is through so-called executive information systems (EIS) and decision support systems (DSS). Computer technology now enables executives not attuned to computer systems or even to the use of the keyboard to call up data from the massive databases held in their companies at the touch of a keypad. These 'naive' users can then massage that data in various ways, including modelling aspects of it in future projections.

Computer literacy is growing rapidly and a new generation of managers is emerging, who have grown up with computers. So it is likely that ten years from now it will be commonplace for executives to have workstations and boardroom facilities, which will enable them to assess and model data electronically.

As a result, we can expect a very rapid growth in the demand for information systems, which make visibility and manipulation of data much easier than they have ever been. There are three or four systems now available in the UK which do just that. The chief characteristic of these systems is their realtime flexibility–you can call up data in any form that you want. These are truly accessible and comprehensive databases of a sort not available even five years ago.

At the moment, only a few very large, blue chip companies are using them and can justify the expenditure. But we shall soon see packages running on personal computers that will do much the same thing for quite small organisations.

The trend to decentralisation means that information systems are absolutely vital, if management is to stay in control. The more you delegate, the more you need effective systems to control and co-ordinate.

A survey by the British Institute of Management (BIM) last year showed that the majority of head offices now include information systems among their responsibilities. (Figure 2.4)

The BIM found that in the more hands-on head offices, information systems are regarded as the most critical staff function carried out there. Most companies also generally agreed it was one of the most difficult staff functions. Information systems staff now typically make up 22–23 per cent of the total employed in head offices.

However, more than half of the BIM survey respondents still regard their information systems as a service to the operating companies and only 14 per cent see them as a means of management control. This shows that there is a long way to go before the importance of EIS is widely understood.

FOCUS ON THE RELEVANT INFORMATION

The second cause of managerial decision-making failure we referred to was not knowing what questions to ask. One of the great problems in building

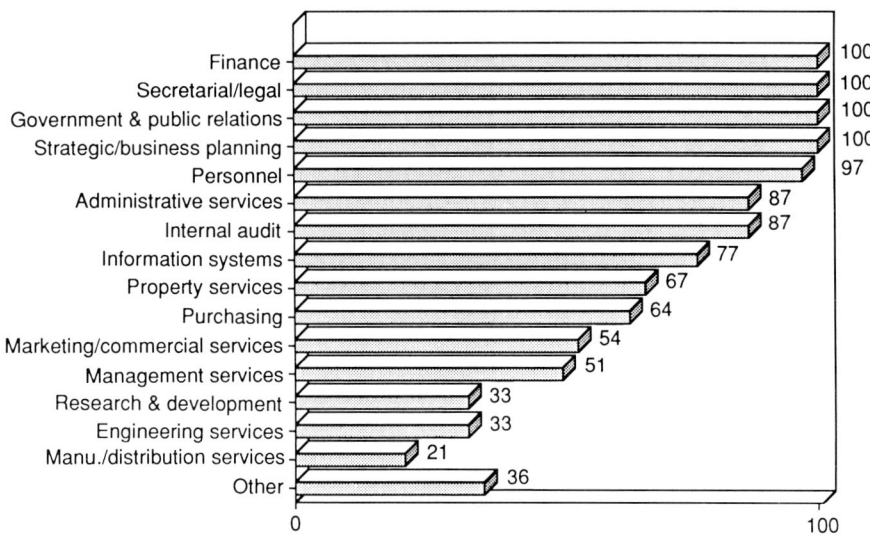

Figure 2.4   Percentage of companies undertaking function at head office (*Source: The Effective Head Office*, British Institute of Management/CRESAP, 1988. Management House, Corby, Northants. *Reproduced by permission*)

information systems has been the inability of the users to say what it is they need to know to run their business more effectively. This still is a problem. There has been a tendency to gather too much information without selectivity; managers are under enormous pressure to read too much and therefore they now question why it is being collected and what they are supposed to do with it. Far too many information systems have been suffocating and not tuned to inducing self-management and self-discipline. Boards of directors have no easy or clearly defined way of using information to make the business more effective, because very often the duties and modus operandi of boards have not been set out clearly enough.

There is no doubt that information technology will make an enormous contribution to making management information gathering, manipulation and visibility much more effective. The data is there, the technology is there; what it demands now is a different attitude in the boardroom to the subject of information.

THE HUMAN DIMENSION

Undoubtedly these new technologies will make management more effective, but we must not forget the human factor. Earlier, we noted that managing directors were spending a great deal more time on human communications.

We must not let the availability of technology systems make us overlook the prime importance of talking to people.

An excellent Rank training film about the so-called 'GOYA effect' told the story of a numerate, systems-minded man, who was appointed to a general management position and felt that the way to run business was by charts, graphs and statistics. But to his horror all the various indicators of sales, staff turnover, and the rest began to move in the wrong direction. In desperation he turned to an 'old soldier' and said, 'what shall I do about all this?' and the man said 'what you need is the GOYA effect: Get Off Your Arse and go out and see!'

It is no good having the most effective information systems in the world if the top managers do not get out and about in their own operations and in the marketplace. This is the only way in which they can bring the statistics to life with direct experience of what is happening–an attitude aptly summarised by my colleague Roger Graham as 'having one's head out of the window'–and by the way, the Tiger Moth was one of the world's most successful aircraft!

3

MANAGING WITH INFORMATION SYSTEMS: EFFECTIVENESS OR EFFICIENCY?

'As information management becomes increasingly critical for achieving and maintaining competitive advantage, top management is of necessity more involved. Among the major concerns is how to ensure that information systems truly support the key business objectives – that they are effective rather than merely efficient. The answer,' says Garf Collins, Managing Director, BIS Applied Systems, 'lies in creating an information strategy that comprehends and makes use of the variety of approaches now available.'

When people talk of 'managing with information systems', all too often they mean *getting by* with inadequate systems rather than *controlling* their information needs. In too many companies, the systems are wrong for the objectives of the business, weak in their functions and prone to failure. Business success today is increasingly dependent upon information systems based on computers and networks which give support to the critical functions of the organisation.

Over the last decade emphasis has moved from improving operational activity to the creation of systems which affect the destiny of the organisation. These 'mission-critical' systems are bound up with the effectiveness of the organisation. Effectiveness is critical. It is all too easy for an organisational activity to be very efficient, while striving towards the wrong objectives.

In the pursuit of these mission-critical systems, major management concerns have arisen about both effectiveness and efficiency. The solution to these problems proposed by the software community has been 'software engineering'. This discipline attempts to make the building of systems into an engineering science with the standards, predictability and reliability of the best traditional engineering practice.

Can software engineering really help management to achieve its objectives in a way that benefits the whole organisation, rather than simply achieve efficiency within the information systems department? The following brief survey of some practical cases provides some of the answers and illustrates how diverse the approaches to system building can be.

CASE 1: THE DEPARTMENT OF HEALTH AND SOCIAL SECURITY

The Department of Health and Social Security in the UK is building one of the largest systems in the world. It will link all Social Security and Department of Employment offices through a single network into a co-ordinated database.

In such a system, the technical complexity is matched by the organisational challenge. The system has to serve many sections of a vast organisation. It has to deliver the requirements of management, which includes politicians, senior civil servants and diverse operational managers. It also has to provide benefit to its 'shareholders' and consumers, that is the general public.

Systems like this, where no one part of the organisation, is the sole sponsor, have to be regarded as being owned by the whole organisation. Let us call them 'corporate systems'. Often, as in this case, they require a complex and unique system, built specially for the needs of one organisation.

CASE 2: A MAJOR BANK

The bank set up an investment management organisation as a separate company. Investment management is one of the most complex fields in financial services. It deals with many different sorts of investment vehicle in multiple currencies and manages funds at a variety of strategic and tactical levels.

To build a dynamic and rapidly expanding new organisation, and at the same time create a complex new information system to support it, is a considerable challenge. It would have been hard to achieve with traditional system development methods.

The process of analysing and designing the requirements for the system was cut short by using a novel approach. It took as a starting point a fully defined investment management system held within an automated system development 'workbench'–a system developer's set of tools. It quickly adapted that system to suit its precise requirements, enabling the developers to move much more quickly to implement the system, than they could otherwise have done.

Unlike the DHSS corporate system, this one had characteristics similar to those used by other organisations and therefore was able to benefit from the modern equivalent of a software package.

CASE 3: GUINNESS

Guinness is a company renowned for its marketing expertise. It is developing a well considered and well-structured information systems strategy, to serve the whole of the organisation. An important part of that strategy is to support marketing through intelligent use of information technology.

But even in such circumstances, there arise needs which have to be satisfied very quickly. Just such a need arose when the export department wanted a system to support its marketing activities. It used one of the latest programming languages—one of the Fourth Generation Languages (4GLs)—to cut the time and effort spent in programming.

Its approach was to define an elapsed time and amount of effort, commensurate with the benefits of the system. A small team then developed the system requirements with the users. They produced reports using the 4GL, which were then refined in discussion to reflect the users' needs more accurately. The management of a department requiring such a system has to be continuously aware of how it is using its limited resource, so it can deliver first those system functions which are of the highest priority. This type of concentration is healthy and can increase the sense of commitment and ownership by the users and their management.

CASE 4: PROFESSIONAL SERVICES

The finance director of a professional services company, has distilled a number of measures of performance of the organisation down to a few key factors, which he monitors closely. However, he is frustrated by the fact that many of these numbers are embedded in prolific output from information systems and the appropriate ratios and comparisons are not projected in suitably crisp form.

Having decided to remedy this situation, the financial director was astounded by the huge estimate for a conventional systems project. This would have entailed rewriting a large part of the operational systems to deliver the small amount of information he needed.

He then talked to a consultant, who suggested a more pragmatic approach, using some ready-made software tools available on the mainframe computer to extract the information needed and present it in an attractive graphical form. The director received a system, but found it too cumbersome to use, since it required him to know too much about the working of the software. Moreover, its physical performance was poor.

Three years after his quest started he came across a small personal computer package which seemed able to do the job. He persuaded the computer people to produce for him a few files in the right format and within a few weeks of spare-time work at last had his key performance factors system.

THE TYPES OF SYSTEM

The lesson of these examples is that there is no single approach to developing systems, which is appropriate for all circumstances. So how does one choose the right approach and what types of system are available?

The cases quoted illustrate some types, but not all. Figure 3.1 shows a classification of systems and their expected relative popularity over a period of time.

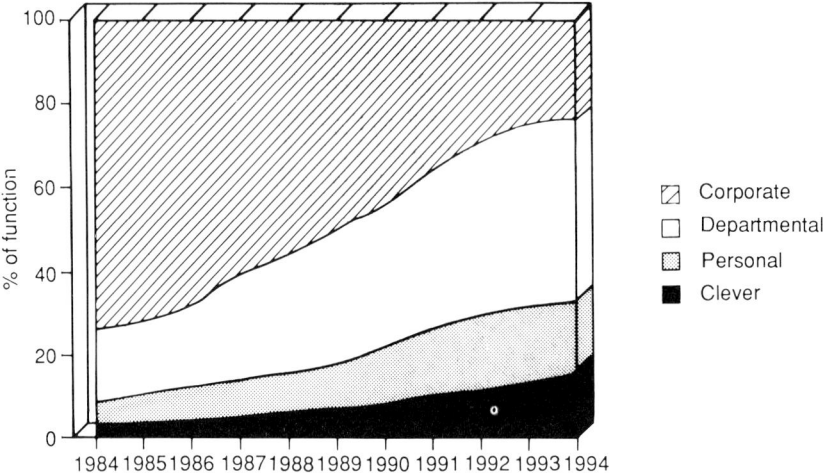

Figure 3.1   Styles of system

Corporate systems

These serve the requirements of many different user functions, usually across several departments of the organisation. The data, which these systems hold, is shared by a variety of users and no single line of management is completely responsible for them. Often, as a result of this, the systems are large and complex, both in their business function and the technology which delivers it. Although declining relatively, this type of system will still grow in absolute volume.

Departmental systems

These serve the needs of a single function in an organisation, for example, a sales information system or a production monitoring system. These systems exchange information with other systems, but they have a scope of requirement, which falls substantially within this single function and are therefore called departmental systems. They are also easy to run on computers dedicated to that application.

Personal systems

These deal with information particular to an individual. They may draw on data from elsewhere, but do not change it at source. They use ready-made software to create rapidly an application system for that user. Very often such systems are based on microcomputers and their associated software, but there are also facilities on mainframe computers for individuals to create their own systems.

'Clever' systems

These can share characteristics with any of the previous three types. But they are primarily aimed at replacing or increasing professional expertise. These are by far the newest sort of system and they have unfortunately got bound up with the technical computing concept of 'expert systems'.

For years, there have been systems using approaches other than 'expert systems', which have achieved the same objective of enhancing professional expertise, for example, complex production scheduling or routing of vehicles for maximising service and minimising cost.

This is a fast-growing, although still small, category which will grow much faster as the software tools supporting such systems become better integrated into conventional systems facilities.

All the last three types of system are expected to grow at the expense of corporate systems. Their growth rate is thus higher than the overall growth rate for software which is approximately 20 per cent per year, as shown in Figure 3.1.

THE COMPUTING STRATEGY

Large companies typically have a proliferation of various systems across the organisation. Because they need these systems to communicate at various levels, these companies are increasingly developing computing strategies. These define the major systems required by the company in outline, lay down the technical shape of the computing and communications facilities and set standards, both for internal systems and for preferred suppliers.

Figure 3.2 illustrates the general case for computing networks.

Technical issues include the argument by some commentators that, because microcomputers are becoming powerful worskstations, they could be simply linked to a large mainframe to interact with huge databases. However, it is likely that many organisations will keep their intermediate machines. One reason for this is that they help to manage departmental data and to provide security and contingency support for departmental systems. Another is that they make it easier to distribute the management of the whole computing complex in a way which fits the organisation generally.

Senior managers are more and more concerned to adopt information and communications standards, which are either formally agreed or *de facto* within the industry. For instance, IMB PC hardware and software standards are now almost universal. Such widely accepted standards improve the compatibility of systems from different suppliers, who are forced away from their proprietory standards as their products become commoditised.

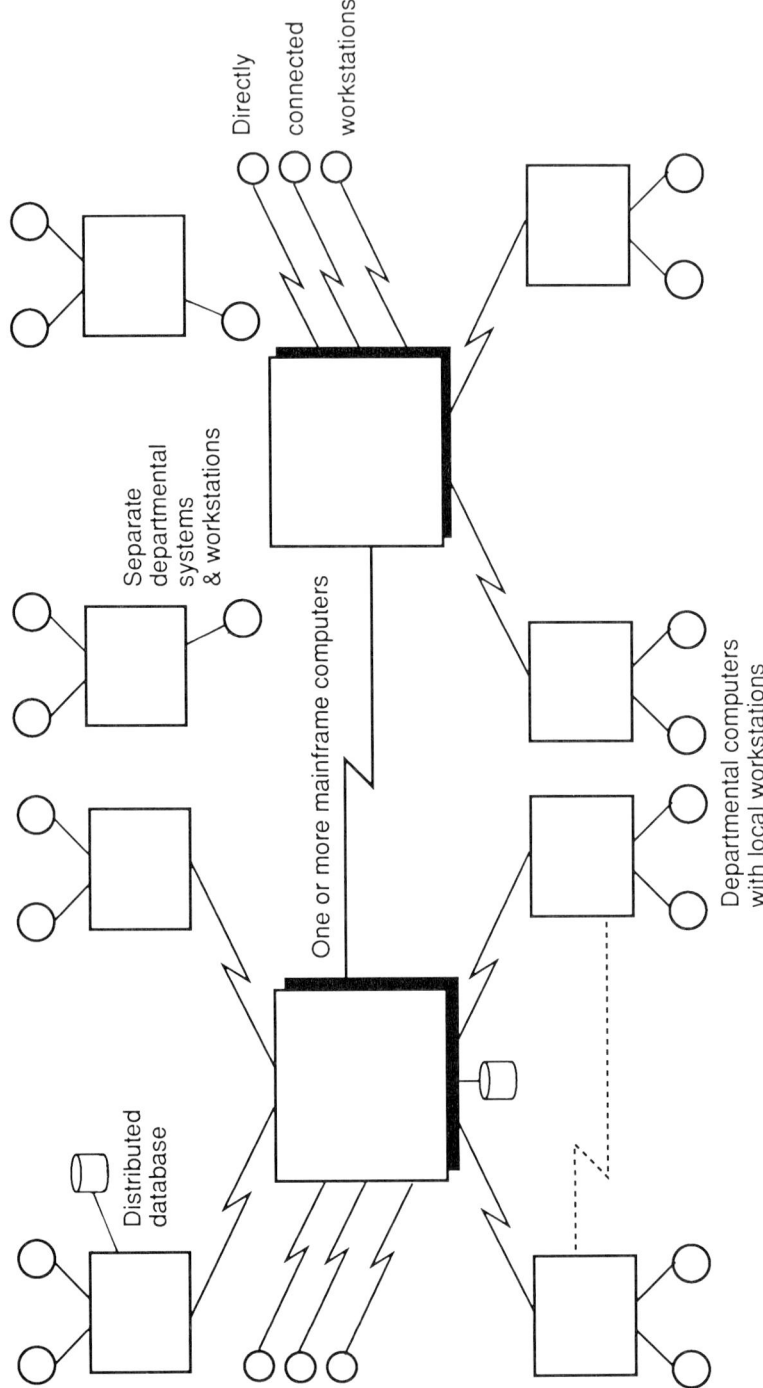

Directly connected workstations

Separate departmental systems & workstations

One or more mainframe computers

Departmental computers with local workstations

Distributed database

Figure 3.2   The computing network

The best managed information systems organisations, establish a strategy that includes these required standards. They plan to deliver applications using all four types of system described above. They recognise the importance of a clear understanding of which systems must be corporate, which ones may be created by departments and whose responsibility it is to ensure cost-benefit in each case. Purchases of departmental, personal and 'clever' systems have to be justified by the benefits of the application and must fall within the standard technical framework.

This attitude to systems provides a powerful combination:

- ensures a high degree of standardisation;
- enhances the potential for compatibility;
- distributes management responsibility for delivering effective systems.

Table 3.1 World market for software and services

	1987	*1991*	*Average % growth*
Processing/networks	35	66	17
Software products	38	95	26
Professional services*	32	66	19
Turnkey systems	19	28	10
Totals	124	255	20

Current distribution: US 49%; Western Europe 27%; Japan 18%; Rest 6%
*Approximately 50% custom software
(*Source* Input)

MANAGING SOFTWARE DEVELOPMENT

The need for companies to have a comprehensive information strategy will increase in line with the continued expansion in demand for both custom and package software (see Table 3.1 which shows the trends in purchases of software and associated services). Organisations will become even more dependent on information systems and will put more and more resources into their creation, acquisition and support.

This presents both an enormous challenge and an opportunity to management. The challenge is to direct this expenditure into 'mission-critical' applications, which are going to affect the destiny of the organisation and mark it out from its competitors. That means avoiding wasting resources by embarking on overcomplicated systems which deliver only efficiency. In many cases a 70 per cent less complex system could deliver 70 per cent of the efficiency.

For public sector organisations, too, phrases such as 'affect the destiny of the organisation' and 'mark it out from its competitors' are becoming increasingly relevant with political change.

Software engineering

A parallel challenge is to seek better and better value for money in the creation and delivery of these systems. This concern, has led to the development of software engineering. Management must grasp these opportunities yet at the same time, it must avoid the excesses caused by the over-enthusiasm of technologists, who sometimes fail to appreciate the objectives of the whole organisation.

Most software engineering techniques use computers to automate activities, which system developers previously did manually. The scope for this can be illustrated by a few examples. A complex system can take as many as 20 000 documents to define precisely what it does. The associated programs may have a million or more lines of code. Just to manage this pile of paper, or hundreds of thousands of screens of information, to organise changes to it and prove its consistency, is a formidable task.

Once such a system is fully defined, users may be asked to consider the suitability of those parts that affect them. Usually they will recommend changes. For instance, a user might point out that customer status has been defined with two meanings, one meaning being credit rating and the other being type of customer. Even if this is a simple correction, it is a daunting task to search 20 000 documents to find all the places where that change affects the system.

Similarly, when dealing with the code in testing or maintaining the system, it is an enormous task to identify the area, which an error may affect and to isolate other parts of the system from the impact of corrections made to correct the error.

Many of the approaches of software engineering are aimed at automating and managing the huge complexity of modern systems in devlopment. They strive to keep complexity away from the system developers, wherever it can be handled autonomously by the support software, for example, in creating code directly from specifications. Only operations, which have been clearly defined can be automated in this way.

Development methodologies

Just as it is pointless trying to develop an application system without a clear view of what is required, so it is also pointless trying to automate the development of systems without knowing what the developers are going to do, the sequence of their tasks and the output they expect.

The definitions of these steps and the techniques which help developers to carry them out, are sometimes called 'development methodologies'. Several of these are popular with computer users and their advocates sometimes sound a bit like evangelists.

Any organisation needs to have a focused approach to methodology so that both users and developers understand how systems come together. The problem is that these methodologies typically deal with only one category of system. They tend to be oriented to corporate systems.

Every methodology is perpetually sniped at by supporters of rivals who claim to have invented a new orthodoxy (e.g. prototyping by which they mean development of systems by experiment and increment). At BIS Applied Systems we have in the 1980s moved very strongly away from the single approach, which was appropriate in the 1970s, to accommodate the multiple approaches which are necessary today.

Table 3.2 represents the costs of ownership of a typical medium-sized to large system which will last for many years, while being adapted to match changes in the organisation and its objectives.

Table 3.2   Cost of ownership

Task	% of cost
System definition and design	23
Programming	13
Testing/implementation	23
Maintenance for 7 years	41
	——
Total	100
Typical corporate system	

From this diagram it is clear that any automated approach, which tackles just programming, is clearly tackling only a small part of the task. A larger part is in the definition and design of the system; a very significant part is in its testing; and the largest, but often least considered part is in the subsequent maintenance.

Table 3.3 summarises some common types of software tools.

New computer languages

The most successful and most widely used to date are the improved languages. Programming went through a number of stages, evolving from very technical 'low level' languages to easier-to-learn third generation languages, chief of which was COBOL, which still accounts for the vast majority of the world's commercial programs.

The new languages, 4GLs, provide much higher level facilities for specifying the processes within programs, for example, requiring the programmer only to point at items to be manipulated and to choose from a list of actions what should be done.

These languages have also provided a much more convenient and logical way of handling data and of changing it as the organisation changes without

Table 3.3 Some tools and methods

Development	System re-engineering
CASE tools	Code restructuring
Fourth generation languages	analysis
COBOL generators	translation
Applications generators	
Query languages	*Management*
PC tools, e.g. LOTUS	Estimating
Expert system shells	Project management
	Quality management
Methodologies	
Strategy	
Development	
Maintenance	

having to change the logic of the programs radically as was necessary before.

Such languages can deliver between 20 per cent and several hundred per cent improvements in programming productivity. Some languages can also produce programs in COBOL automatically from the language written by the programmer, which can run more efficiently than 4GL programs and which maintenance staff may prefer as they are more familiar with COBOL. These languages are often called COBOL generators.

4GLs can be used to create systems interactively with users, an approach often called 'prototyping'. To be successful protoyping can only be used with a fairly simple system and with a few users users who are clear about their requirements. For larger systems a more structured approach is still needed, although prototyping should be used to define and agree parts of the system. Complex systems still require substantial work in analysing and defining the user's needs and turning them into a design which fits the technical environment.

'Workbenches' and expert systems

CASE (Computer Assisted Software Engineering) tools based on personal computers provide some of the facilities for a project worker to carry this out. They assist in creating the logical definition and technical design of the system and sometimes in translating this into the form of a target programming language. The closer such tools get to automatic generation of a range of common programming languages for common types of computer, the closer we will come to achieving truly 'portable' systems.

A weakness of many of these workbenches lies in their inability to link together the many developers who may be involved in a project. Some workbenches can do this well, among them, I would contend, BIS/IPSE, which started from the view that this ability was crucial.

Another important new type of software development tool is the expert systems framework, which enables some 'clever' systems to be developed without the specialist knowledge that would otherwise be necessary. The disadvantage of this group of tools is that they tend to be poorly integrated with the more general tools and therefore cannot easily access corporate data.

These tools are simply some of the most useful in supporting the project management of systems and helping to achieve higher quality. There are many others in a wide range of areas. Yet there are some notable gaps. For example, there are very few tools which attempt to tackle the biggest area of expense. This is the management of live systems, their maintenance and their high level definition. Testing is also barely covered by current technology, as it is complex and hard to achieve automatically. Some of the tools mentioned reduce the amount of testing needed by reducing the opportunity for errors to be introduced, but this improvement has still a long way to go. These less catered-for areas of software need some expert systems of their own; the cobbler's children still suffer the occasional chilblain!

DECISIONS FOR TOP MANAGEMENT

1 *Setting priorities*

It is all too easy to get caught up in the complexities and the religious fervour, which go with these software tools and methods. It is also easy to get sidetracked from the main objectives of the systems, which are to support and advance the objectives of the organisation, to achieve higher productivity and to deliver maintainable and adaptable systems.

I began by arguing that an organisation should seek effectiveness, rather than efficiency. To do this, it is necessary for top management to understand its business processes at the highest level and to set priorities for where systems can be of crucial benefit. It is in setting priorities such as these that the biggest gains in productivity can be acheived. It is self-evident that to spend a certain amount of money on a system fundamental to the organisation's success is far more productive than to spend it on a worthy system, which merely increases slightly the efficiency of one part of the organisation.

Figure 3.3 illustrates some business functions for a commercial organisation.

Although many organisations have similar business functions, they differ widely in their priorities for systems. For example, preparing literature is a

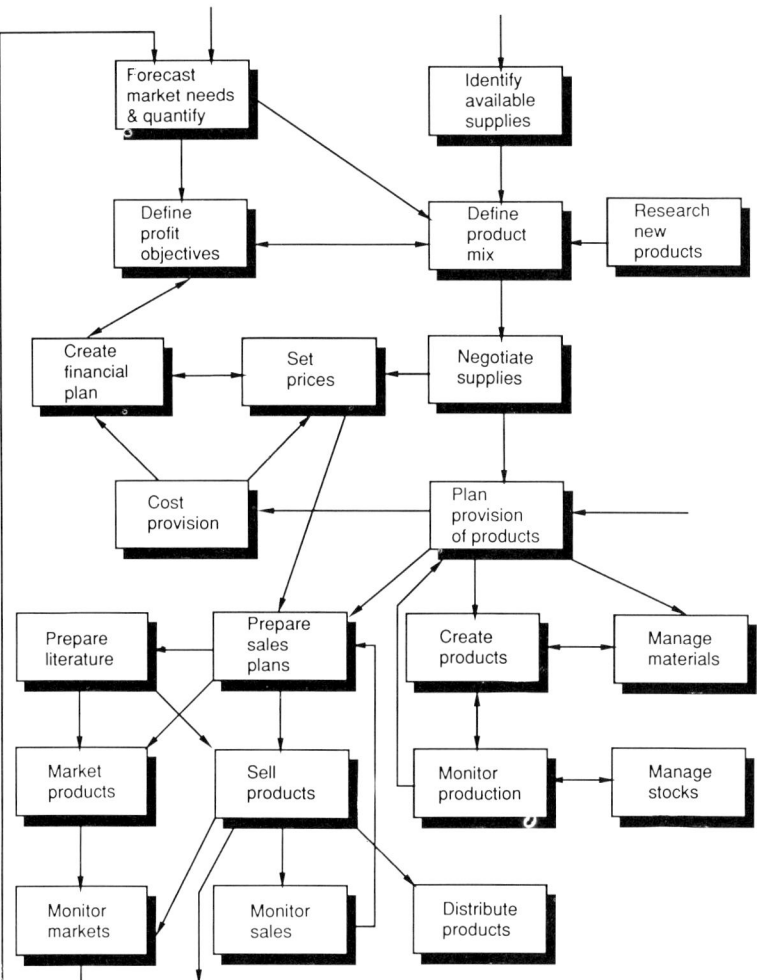

Figure 3.3   Examples of business functions

necessary, but not a mission-critical function for an engine manufacturer yet for a tour operator, it is absolutely crucial. Managing materials may be the crucial function for a company which assembles products from expensive bought-in sub-assemblies. To market and sell products are the most crucial functions of an organisation which provides fast-moving consumer goods, since only the top few brands make profits.

Once top management has decided which systems are mission-critical there is still another crucial set of decisions to be taken on the development approach. This includes how modern software engineering is to be used, what type of system should be created and whether new development can be avoided. Figure 3.4 sets out a process of making these decisions.

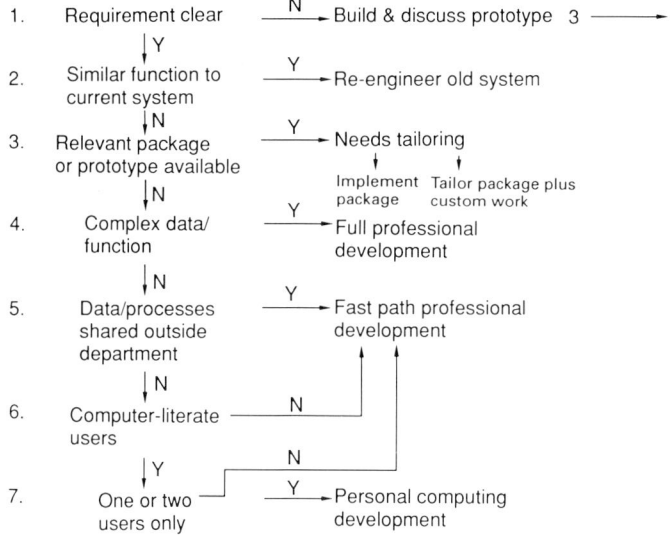

Figure 3.4   A modern development approach

2   *Refurbish or start again?*

The first and rarely considered is to redevelop existing systems. Automated tools are beginning to appear which help this process, but even without these it is still possible. Existing systems, however old-fashioned, are at least a repository of a substantial amount of knowledge of the organisation and its business process. Sometimes, because such systems are deemed unmaintainable and because they lack certain systems functions, they are disregarded and development of a new system starts. The problem is that new system development is inefficient and prone to error, even in reproducing the logic of the old system where it overlaps with the new. If it is not going to be radically different from the old system in its functions, the option of refurbishing the old one should be considered.

There are tools, which can tidy up and redocument existing systems. New input and ouptut sub-systems can be created for the user and the flexibility of input and of information extraction can be improved. All this can be done without changing the core system. Analysis of maintainability might show that the source of the problem is a small number of often-modified programs. These can be reprogrammed, possibly using a 4GL. Perhaps the system can be gradually redeveloped without too much disruption to the users.

3   DIY *versus packages*

Packages have some attractive advantages. Firstly, the code is taken from a supplier, who is responsible for its maintenance. Secondly, the cost of ownership of a package is much lower than that of owning a system developed in house. It is even worth considering changing the way in which the organisation carries out its task to fit a package, so long as it does not interfere with crucial objectives.

Where the fit is not close enough, a package can still form the core of a new system. It may be modified, moderately or even heavily, but it can radically reduce the cost and time for system analysis and design. A package used in this way is fufilling the function sometimes described as a 'systems kernel'. BIS Applied Systems uses a technique called the Automated Business Model (ABM), which works on this principle to speed up the analysis and design stages. The ABM approach enables this interactive adaptation to be done at a logical level before code is written; this is easier for the users to understand and delivers high quality documentation.

THE DEVELOPMENT OPTIONS

Where refurbishment and packages are not appropriate, there are a number of alternative approaches. Figure 3.4 provides further questions top management should ask in making choices of approach to new development.

The first approach, *full professional development*, would be suitable for most corporate systems. The high cost of ownership of such systems and the number of departmental interests demands the highest standards of visible quality. Such systems will still be created with the best traditional practice, but it will be brought up to date by automating some tasks.

Simpler systems, which affect several departments (or for which user skills are not available) can be developed more quickly by using the '*fastpath*' approach. In 'fastpath' development professional developers use a pragmatic subset of the full development procedure. For example, analysis and design can be combined in determining the objectives of the system and its functions can be illustrated by defining the input and output, in the chosen language. Progamming, testing and tuning can be combined into a single phase using a 4GL. The main requirement for 'fastpath' development is that managers should adopt a simple approach and must realise that this technique carries the risk of reducing the system's longevity.

Where the system's impact is within one department and the right user skills exist, users should be encouraged to develop the system directly. By tailoring the approach in this way, the cost of new development can be substantially reduced.

'Clever' systems follow the same decision process as illustrated in Figure 3.4. Within this type of system, many expert systems are now being created using a 'fastpath' approach on micros.

With this wealth of different approaches to development, which are all needed in the modern world, it might be concluded that the term 'software engineering' was a misnomer. As its proponents talk about it, it seems to suggest complex custom system building–a very narrow definition. The term 'information engineering' is commonly used to overcome this impression of narrowness. A more pragmatic description would be 'computer application engineering' because, although the information content is important, users still see the process as the engineering of computer systems to deliver their applications.

SUMMARY

Let me re-cap the guidelines which emerge from all this:

- Get the system strategy right so that development focuses on mission-critical systems.
- Create a compatible technical framework for equipment and software, to cut out non-productive conversion of systems and data and duplicated training.
- Avoid new development where possible. System refurbishment or using packages can reduce the risk and cost substantially.
- If you need a new system, select the approach to match its scale and expected lifetime.
- Apply the best current automated methods such as 4GLs and CASE tools.
- Measure the effect of your approach and adapt it in the light of experience, fitting in new tools and approaches as they become available.

Organisations that follow these guidelines find that their effectiveness is now increasingly dependent on how they use their application systems. As a result, the management of those systems and the choice of a development approach become of great significance to top management. There is no need to wait for the ultimate in systems development automation; major benefits can be achieved with existing techniques. Good management can yield large improvements in cost-benefit.

In the future, new tools and methods will offer greater portability of systems, so that a system developed for one technical environment can easily be converted for use in another. This will result from the spread of generic standards for communication and programming languages. But there will still be systems choices for managers to make. The cost of producing applications will never fall to the same degree as the cost of the basic hardware and software on which they run. Nonetheless, the approaches I have outlined, which are useable now, can deliver large improvements in the cost of the total system.

I have presented systems building as a management concern rather than a technical concern. As the mystique of computing and communications evaporates, it will become steadily more so. The greatest hope for the future is that more and more managers will take up this challenge and will have the self-confidence to make effective use of information systems by determining the mission-critical applications and building the necessary technical resources.

Efficiency, yes–but first, effectiveness.

4

THE ELECTRONICS
INDUSTRY TOMORROW

'Tomorrow may never come for some European electronics companies, if they fail to achieve the economies of scale necessary to compete globally', says Mike Gordon, Chairman and Managing Director, BIS Mackintosh. 'Rapid change in the competitive environment poses an innovation challenge to electronics manufacturers, telecommunications companies, information consultants and software suppliers alike.'

Technology is the principal driver in the electronics industry. The market, the industry and governments all react to relentlessly changing technology and will continue to do so for the foreseeable future. There is still a large gap between what technology can achieve in theory, according to our knowledge of physics, and what is currently realisable in R&D laboratories (or, more importantly, on factory floors).

With current technology we can make chips of one micron, one millionth of a metre. With some more investment we will soon be able to make chips of 0.5 micron and in the longer term we will get down to 0·05 micron, as has already been demonstrated by IBM in the laboratory.

The 0·5-micron chip would give at least a fourfold improvement in

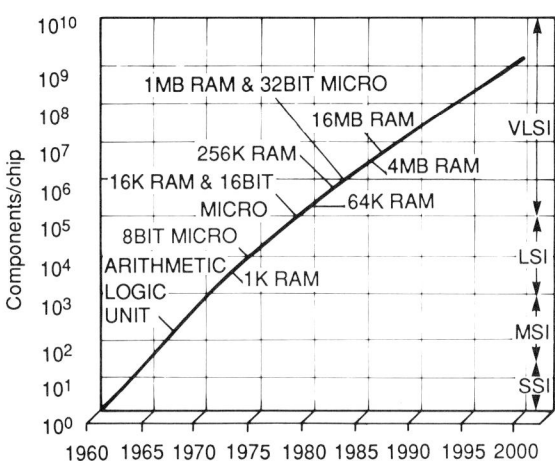

Figure 4.1   Filling the technology gap

Figure 4.2   The ever-reducing costs of electronic functions performed by integrated circuits

performance and the 0·05 micron would give a 400 times improvement. So there is a wide gap between what we know we could achieve with chips and what we have accomplished so far.

The same can be said of a number of major areas of research, such as:

- artificial intelligence (AI), which is only just now beginning to realise its promise. Neural networks which are being developed as part of AI are also theoretically feasible but not yet realisable in practice;
- optical computing – computing using light signals instead of electronics – has been demonstrated in the laboratory but needs much more work before it will deliver increases in the speed of logic;
- molecular circuitry – biological circuits where changes in chemical states will eventually yield the same phenomena as changes in electronic states do at the moment.

These are just some of the leading edge technologies still to be exploited, which will deliver much denser circuitry, more function per square inch and very much faster performance working in picoseconds instead of nanoseconds.

THE BENEFITS OF SIZE

Each advance requires expensive research and development. It is commonly said that to introduce a major telecommunications switch requires at least $1 billion in development funds.

Thirty years ago I worked on gallium arsenide. It has taken 30 years for gallium arsenide to be presented significantly in the marketplace. Some of the developments that are being worked on in the laboratory now will take another 30 years. They will deliver the benefits of smaller and faster circuitry and therefore will bring great commercial gains to the people who can exploit them. But before that can happen very large sums must be invested.

This investment is now best done through joint projects. So two big companies Philips, and Siemens, have got together to invest over $1.5 billion to develop a new random access memory of a higher capacity. Large firms in this market which must run many projects parallel for sustained growth, typically have to invest around 10 per cent of their revenues in R&D, so it takes a company of at least $10 billion in revenues to achieve a single major technology breakthrough each year.

Small may in many things be beautiful, but in electronics big is absolutely necessary. To achieve this size, major electronics firms are looking for more and more acquisitions and mergers. One of the most spectacular examples of growth by acquisition is that of Thomson of France, as is detailed in the illustration in Table 4.1.

Table 4.1   Mergers and acqusitions: consumer electronics

1979		1988
Nordmende	FRG	
SABA	FRG	
Dual	FRG	
Telefunken	FRG	Thomson France
Mostek	USA	
SGS	Italy	
Ferguson	UK	
RCA	USA	
Salora	Finland	
Luxor	Sweden	Nokia Finand
Oceanic	France	
SEL	FRG	

The next 30 years will see major changes in all the information industries, and particularly in computing and telecommunications as they draw closer together. Those changes will be especially evident in the competitive environment that these organisations face. Let us look at some of these in more detail:

The competitive environment in electronics

This trend will continue and intensify as companies need to raise more R&D money to gain a technological edge over their competitors. Western companies are looking closely at the strategy of their Japanese competitors, some of which—Hitachi, Mitsubishi, NEC, Fujitsu—are so big that in some niches of electronics they provide their own internal marketplaces. This means that they can start a product and get initial trials of it on almost a commerical level without ever going outside their own doors.

Now these Japanese companies are being imitated in Korea by similar companies, Goldstar, Samsung, Dai woo and Hyundai, all of which are not only electronics producers but also makers of other products that incorporate electronics and information technology.

Western companies have until recently tended to remain independent and specialised, treating only components or only one facet of a system. They now find they must get together to rival the scale of the Far Eastern companies. This will be an increasing trend in the future.

Europe has created a fragmented, small-scale industry because each of its 12 nations champions its own electronics industry. The Single European Market Act due to come into force in 1992 is an indication that Europe has recognised the problem and is now about to take action. It could well produce some very much bigger companies.

Fragmenting demand

While the supply side is consolidating, the demand side is, paradoxically, fragmenting, with the market now calling for more personalised products. The day of what IBM calls 'the glass house'—a computer room surrounded by glass—is on the wane. All of us can now have on our desks micros, which have the equivalent power of a mainframe of just a few years ago. The computer on our desk will grow in power and it will soon be accompanied not only by our own telephone but also maybe our own videophone and by our own personal fax machine. The personalisation of electronics products will grow and the consumer will increasingly demand the same basic configuration of electronic products around him whether he is in the office or at home or travelling in a car or even by air. (Figure 4.3)

This of course implies a rapidly changing market, of increasingly higher volume as electronics products are sold more and more to individuals rather than organisations. Companies will have to place greater emphasis on marketing skills to make maximum use of the distinguishing features of new products and of new distribution mechanisms. In this environment the winners will be the companies with the most effective distribution mechanisms.

The market shift to high personal demand will thus coincide with the need for high volume flexible production to justify the costs of R & D.

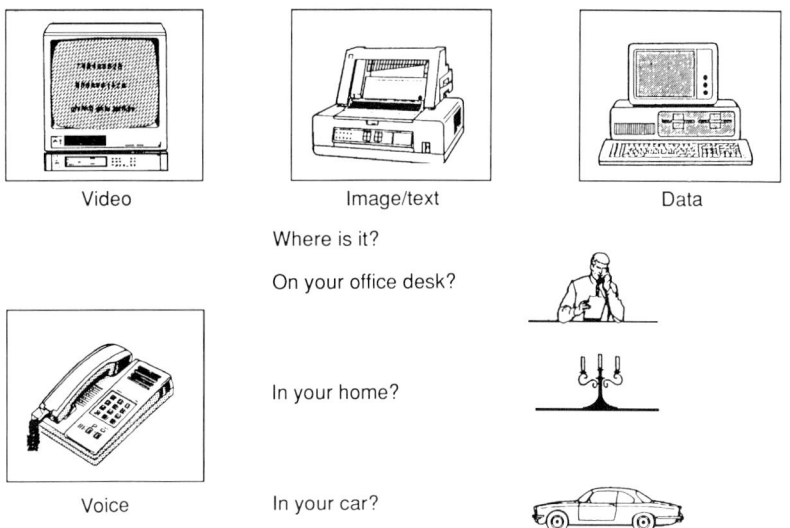

Figure 4.3 Personalisation of products

Networking and user friendliness

Another implication of these trends is that, with lots of individuals using many different electronic products, networking–individuals able to contact one another with minimal personal intervention with electronic devices and with the user having to take the minimum number of actions–will spread. It is safe to predict that it will continue apace for at least the next 20 years.

The problem of achieving user-friendliness, which currently inhibits networking, is not going to be solved in a short time. The development of ISDN (the integrated digital services network), was conceived as a technical solution to a variety of telecommunications problems, including networking but it is also fuelled by the need to make networking devices more friendly.

The ultimate objective of ISDN is to try to make all of the devices work from only one outlet. Ideally, all of the devices will be crammed into just one machine, combining voice, data, text and video, and the ability to process the signals associated with each. (Figure 4.4)

Experts talk about this problem of user-friendliness as the man-machine interface. Developments in broadband ISDN are addressing this problem by allowing communication by moving pictures. Networks are increasingly more than just fibres and copper coaxial or twisted pair cables. 'Virtual networks' are emerging, created by software. This thrust into networks will eventually cause an expansion in software for telecommunications.

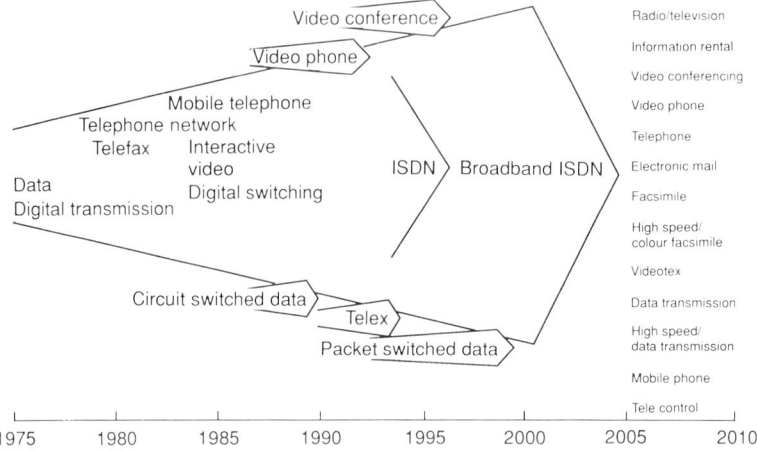

Figure 4.4   The inexorable advance of the integrated services digital network

The impact on suppliers

One characteristic of software companies has been that they are small enterprises which grow very quickly and are often bought by the bigger companies. This trend of acquisition and merger will also continue, for the same reason as happened on the hardware side, namely that to justify high R&D costs software will have to serve a global market. Consolidation of software companies is already evident. In the next 10–15 years the marketplace will fall out into 10–20 very big companies and a large number of small specialist companies.

The survival of a multitude of small companies, both in hardware and software, would seem to contradict my contention that the future lies with big companies, but the anomaly is easily explicable. Big companies have to make big investments, so in the interests of their shareholders they should not move too quickly. They use their shareholders' money to invest in R&D and to equip themselves for large-scale production so they cannot suddenly change to take on board the latest small development.

What they will tend to do therefore is inadvertently, by virtue of their understandable slowness, to encourage people in their R&D laboratories to take a particular development, leave the mother company and set up a smaller, faster organisation not committed to supporting worldwide distribution. This spin-off venture can then develop for a local market. When the small company succeeds in developing its local market, the big company comes back on to the scene and acquires it. This process has been happening in the US. The role of the small company should therefore really be seen as a sub-set of the big company, not a trend in the opposite direction.

As electronic circuitry becomes smaller and smaller, it uses less and less material and material costs fall. It is no longer possible to process it manually, so it has to be processed by automated or robotic means. This applies not only to manufacturing, but design and testing. So labour costs as well as material costs fall.

That leaves only processing cost and overheads. Processing costs are quite low, so the main cost comes in capital investment. The principal cost components here are investment in R&D, in robots to handle miniature circuitry, in clean factories (chip manufacturers) and stable factories (they are even talking about building factories on geologically stable foundations because the circuitry cannot tolerate the minutest tremors in the earth). Compared with this enormous expenditure materials and labour cease to be a consideration.

At the same time, incidentally, there will have to be completely new thoughts on how to run the books of accounts. The way accountants treat industry at present is often antediluvian. The marginal cost of production of the piece of circuitry as we have seen is actually quite low. Break-even levels are determined by the point at which sales revenues equal the fixed costs of production. This phenomenon will force more careful treatment of those 'fixed' costs.

THE COMPETITIVE ENVIRONMENT IN TELECOMMUNICATIONS

The rapid progress of technology and its effect on public policy has made government see the need for ending the monopolistic practices of the electronics industry, particularly in telecommunications. Deregulation is clearly a response to failure by these monopolies to provide an adequate level of service to the public.

The divestiture of AT&T brought on equally radical changes at British Telecom, in the Japanese NTT and will draw in the West German Bundespost and France Telecom. Governments all over the world are getting out of the way, taking off the regulations. Telecommunications in the US began the deregulation movement for all the other industries worldwide.

Telecommunications as a regulated quasi-governmental sector tended to be the neglected part of the electronics industry. When people quoted the revenue of the electronics industry they frequently left off the amount of money generated by telecommunications traffic. Yet its more than $350 billion revenues worldwide dwarfs those of any other sector of the industry.

All the trends of the electronics industry, such as increased personalisation of products and increased networking, will serve to grow telecommunications traffic. The power of the telecommunications companies, liberated from the restraining hand of government, will therefore also increase. These major telecommunications companies have a natural interest in becoming significant players in software because software serves their basic industry by adding value to communications. So they could soon occupy key positions in the information technology industry alongside IBM and DEC.

THE COMPETITIVE ENVIRONMENT IN INFORMATION-BASED CONSULTANCY

An increasingly important sub-sector of the electronics industry is information-based consultancy. Some major consultancies now have hundreds of millions of dollars of revenues. The nature of consultancy is also rapidly changing. No

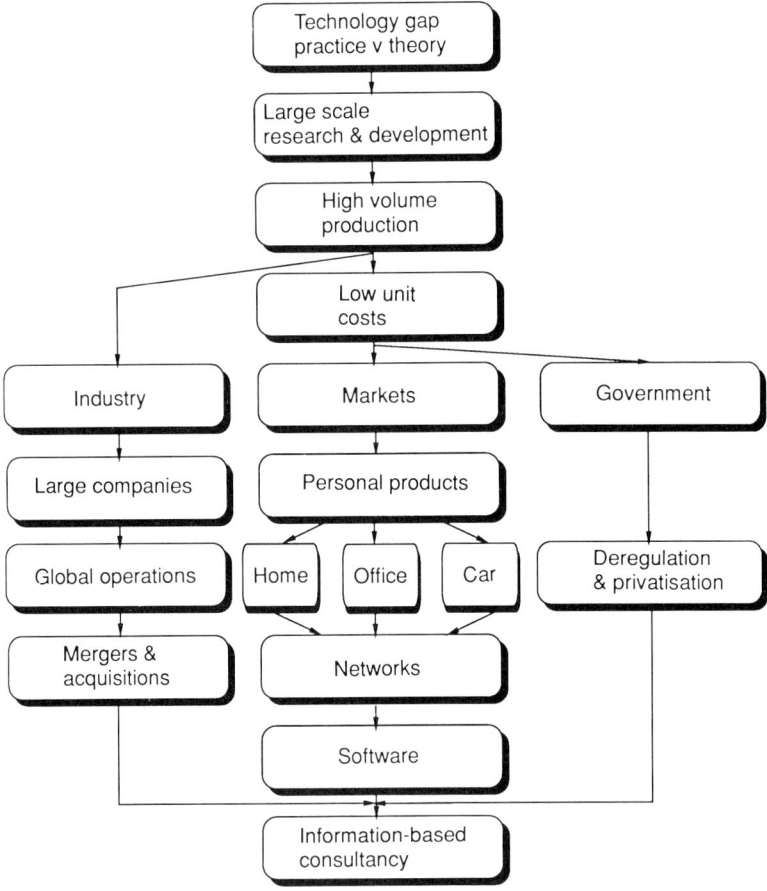

Figure 4.5   Present and future market drivers: electronics and information technology

longer can a consultant come in to a company, study the facts and figures and produce a report to the management with conclusions and recommendations. Now the top executive expects to have the consultant's detailed information available at the moment when he needs it to make his own decision. Consultants are now being challenged by their customers to produce the factual evidence on which their recommendations are based.

Information-based consultancy will be demanded in two forms:

- the high-priced, company-specific information for top level, corporate decisions;
- the publications bought by the individual from the bookstall in magazine form to allow him to keep up to date with all those new electronic gadgets that appear on his desk, his dining table and his dashboard.

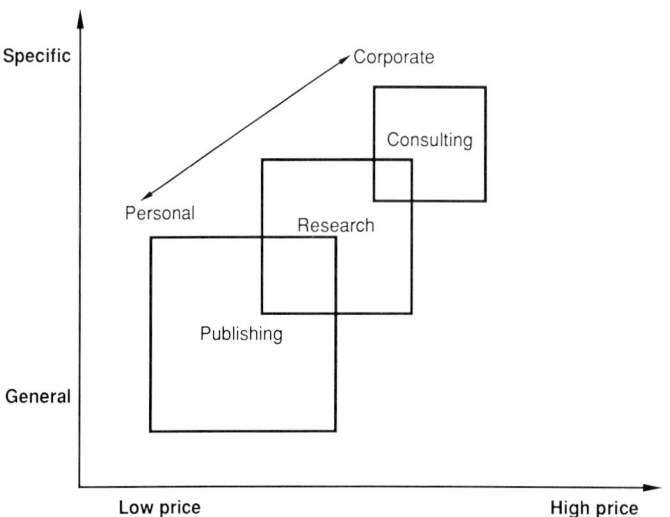

Figure 4.6   The interwoven markets of information provision and consulting

THE COMPETITIVE ENVIRONMENT IN SOFTWARE

The large Far Eastern companies have been making strides in capturing parts of the information industry over the past 20 years and the signs are that they will continue to do so for the next 20 years. Twenty years ago the Japanese were only just entering the consumer electronics industry, threatening RCA, Philips and Thorn-EMI. Now they completely dominate the industry worldwide. The Japanese have virtually taken over the watch industry, the motorcycle industry, shipbuilding and consumer electronics. They are becoming increasingly powerful in the chip industry, now holding the top three places in the league table, having been nowhere ten years ago.

The notion that the Japanese are by nature copiers rather than inventors and are therefore not capable of writing good software is demonstrably untrue. A company such as Fujitsu has more than a dozen separate software departments and is making enormous progress. The Japanese have a well laid-out plan for the development of ISDN which will put a fibre in every Japanese home by the year 2000, well in advance of any other country in the world. That development will be extensively based on Japanese software for the switching and processing signals.

It is all too easy for Western companies to underestimate the national sense of purpose, the dedication of resources and the creativity of the Japanese and Korean industries. Both now use the world's most sophisticated production engineering techniques for both hardware and software.

I visited a factory in Japan recently which, through the use of computer-integrated manufacturing, has increased ouptut of optical card readers over a period of five years by a factor of eight, while reducing labour by between 10 per cent and 15 per cent. That's close to a productivity increase of ten times. One of the key elements in this strategy was a form of computer integrated manufacturing (CIM) that relies heavily on their own indigenous software.

THE INNOVATION CHALLENGE

Any remaining doubts about Japanese creativity can be dispelled by examining the number of Japanese patent registrations in the United States. From 2625 in 1970 the number has risen to 13 209 in 1986. The US and UK levels of registrations have meanwhile been declining and there have been only modest increases in France, West Germany and Italy. Japan is rapidly outstripping any other country in inventiveness.

Unless there is a concerted movement to meet the deliberate thrust by the industries of Japan, Korea and Taiwan, (who are supported by Hong Kong and

Table 4.2 The Pacific winner. US patents granted: by country of origin

	Percentage increase/(reduction) in US patents granted 1970 to 1986 (%)
Japan	400
West Germany	53
France	26
Canada	23
Switzerland	8
United Kingdom	(18)
United States	(19)

Singapore), the future winners are going to come from the Pacific Rim. Many of these companies have the necessary scale already, so they do not need to make further acquisitions to succeed. It is the Europeans who need to develop the political will to get competing companies together and create the critical mass.

Our company, BIS Mackintosh, has advocated the establishment of a Europe-wide grid which would bring fibre optics into the vast majority of the homes and businesses in the densely populated London–Paris–Bonn triangle, a telecommunications network across national frontiers which could win the approval of many of the commercial organisations and the PTTs involved. But for that to happen it would require political leadership on a European level.

Government has a vital role to play here. It was government which split up AT&T; government and industry work hand-in-glove in Japan. European governments must now create the climate for major players to emerge on the world scene.

5

THE INFORMATION INDUSTRY: A TRILLION DOLLAR TOMORROW

'Both suppliers and users of information technology face major challenges in achieving sustainable competitive advantage. An understanding of the processes at work and effective planning procedures are critical', say Dr Gad J. Selig, Vice President and General Manager, NYNEX Information Solutions Group and Harvey L. Poppel, partner of Broadview Associates.

Information technology (IT) has penetrated to the core of our personal and professional lives. In this chapter we want to look at IT from two perspectives, that of the supplier and that of the user, to see what the future may hold for each.

On the supplier side the information technology industry is a fusion of numerous business sectors—computer equipment and software, information systems, systems integration, telecommunications and systems networks, publishing, entertainment, consumer electronics and others, which until recently were only casually related, if at all.

The users are equally underdeveloped in their approach to IT products and services. Most organisations have still not adjusted their practices, management styles and attitudes to take full advantage of IT. Many are only just beginning to consider information as a resource. They have still to understand that IT, if carefully planned and effectively implemented, can provide major opportunities for generating revenue and cutting costs. Indeed, they may have so undervalued their information that they have made inadequate plans for ensuring its security or for handling a computer disaster.

Most corporate accounting systems are not yet set up to capture detailed information resource management (IRM) expenses. IRM planning—the management of present and future computing and telecommunication systems and resources—is a very difficult exercise, so most businesses that have embarked on it, have tended to focus on short-term rather than medium- or long-term advantages. Plans tend to concentrate on equipment, rather than on new telecommunications opportunities and value-added information services. In addition, few IRM plans are integrated with business planning processes. As

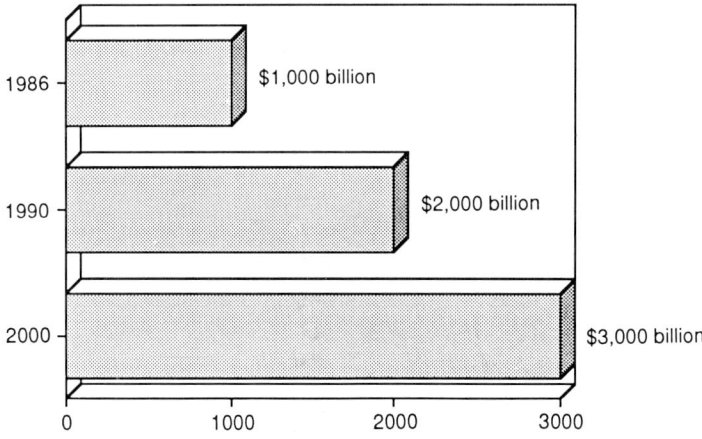

Figure 5.1 Estimated worldwide expenditure on IT

a result, they lack strong support from senior executives. Even in the more sophisticated organisations the concept of the chief information officer is only just emerging.

Without a central responsibility, IRM remains a fragmented activity in most organisations. This lack of formal planning and co-ordination in turn means that the organisation has not evolved a clear and formalised way of planning, monitoring and control. Without such standards, practices of environmental data gathering tend to be poor and people's responsibilities are unclear. If all this were not enough, IRM suffers from a severe shortage of qualified personnel. In sum, IRM is undervalued, understaffed and generally not effectively utilised.

Nonetheless, many large businesses, both in the public and private sectors, are now beginning to grasp how important IT is to their success. They are spending much more on IT, with a good deal of that investment going towards developing the internal systems, procedures, networks and structures that will allow them to use IT in a strategic manner. (Figure 5.1)

Half of the projected expenditure in 1990 is likely to be both produced and consumed in North America. For example, many companies worldwide now realise that there are vast improvements in administrative productivity and profitability to be gained through effective and focused automation.

THE CHALLENGE FOR VENDORS

Surging demand has brought fiercely fought market contests among businesses that develop, produce and distribute IT. Suppliers fall into six categories or clusters (Table 5.1).

Table 5.1 IT clusters

Services	Products
Communications	Consumer electronics
Information	Office equipment
Entertainment	Business operations

As competition intensifies, no IT supplier, no matter in which cluster, however large or seemingly entrenched, is secure. Today's winners can easily be tomorrow's losers. The mid-1980s slowdown in demand for general computers and voice communications equipment humbled even some of the most successful and self-confident players. But at the same time there is increased demand for professional services, software, systems integration and data communications. Therefore suppliers who intend to survive must include these segments in their future products and services.

The clusters on the service side will be invaded by powerful product suppliers in search of higher returns on equity, higher market share, greater stability and more value-added. These suppliers will elbow their way in by their strengths in new technology, excellent marketing and rigorous management disciplines– all qualities, which are often lacking among traditional service suppliers.

The service clusters will not be defenceless, however. Each still has many opportunites both to defend its territory and to expand in its own way. One example may be for a traditional communications services company like NYNEX to expand into the information systems and software area. Moreover, the product clusters will have troubles of their own. They will continue to be affected by shortening product life-cycles and by technology 'leapfrogging', while customers become more IT-literate and discriminating. The cumulative effect of these trends will be sharper up-and-down sales cycles.

Product differentiation based on sheer power will be increasingly difficult to assert. Marketing, delivery, full service and pricing strategies will become the elements which make the difference between prosperity and disaster. Distinctions among product clusters will continue to blur. The quest for differentiation and compatibility with other products will become critical and will create a shift from in-house to external development.

The IT vendors will have to cope with five dominant trends:

- value added
- compatibility (interoperability)
- direct selling
- globalisation
- convergence

Value-added

Value-added–the intangible increase in value that comes from adding to hardware applications such as custom software, training, databases, systems integration and support systems–is gaining strategic importance at the expense of raw computer power, storage and transmission capacity.

Contrary to Marshall McLuhan's famous assertion, that 'the medium is becoming the message', the importance of the message or information content is transcending that of the medium or hardware. Increasingly IT-literate end-users are discovering that appropriate and well-crafted content endures far longer than any particular media. For example, the voice of Caruso, the opera singer, will outlive the vinyl records which made his name. The technologies which drive the media encourage the creation and distribution of new value-added. For instance, interactive electronic training and marketing materials were inspired by advances in laser discs.

Technology is cutting the costs of most media. But meanwhile value-added is rising in cost, largely because of the rising cost of labour. Knowledge workers and creative people are increasingly scarce and expensive resources. So too is their environment, including offices, computer-aided design workstations and software. However, fifth generation software and computer aided systems engineering tools (CASE) will reduce the time for knowledge workers to be more productive through automation.

Compatibility (interoperability)

Delivering value-added increasingly demands compatibility (or interoperability) and interconnectivity of systems and networks. Compatibility in this context means the ability of two or more parties, machine or human, to make a perfect communication; 'perfect' means with no perceptible distortion or unintended delay between the origination of the contents, its processing and end-use. Exchanges between people become 'perfect' by eliminating intermediaries, either people or IT, which might filter out subtleties or slow down communication. Anything other than face-to-face is less than perfect because it causes distortions or delays.

In the world of telephones, compatibility means providing universal service and low-noise transmission. What is said at one end must be carried through interconnecting paths to come out clearly at the other, even though you cannot see the other party. We now expect the same quality of reception from a phone call from 10 000 miles away as we do from one made a mile away.

In computers, users find compatibility to be one of the most severe problems they face. The sheer complexity of requirement is becoming overwhelming as more and more people in different places want simultaneous connections with each other and with their machines. And they want this more amd more often, while using a variety of media from different suppliers. Computers, achieve compatibility through high performance systems components, harmonised hardware, software and networks configurations, high-speed data channels and automatic error correction mechanisms. But the diversity of solutions adds its own level of complexity.

The IT user community is becoming more attuned to the problems of compatibility and will demand greater compliance by vendors to standards such as ANSI standard language, ASCII character sets, X.25 telecommunications connections, ISO/OSI networks, PC-DOS and UNIX software operating systems, the CCITT Group 3 digital facsimile and the MAP/TOP local area networks.

Another critical component of compatibility is the creation of common data elements, defined in the form of a data dictionary, between organisations. Without such commonality of language, it becomes difficult to introduce electronic invoicing and payments systems between customer and vendor companies, for example electronic funds transfer systems (EFTS) or point of sale (POS) systems as companies grow and become more decentralised, common data definitions become as important as communications compatibility.

Direct selling

The use of new IT is leading to more nearly perfect markets; that is markets, which minimise the number of intermediate stages between buyer and seller. This will often permit buyers and sellers to conduct transactions more efficiently, accurately and punctually.

In service businesses, agents, tellers, telephone operators and teachers may be among the endangered species of intermediaries if they do not add sufficient value. Even physical intermediaries such as warehouses, travel agents, retail stores and outpatient rooms can sometimes be bypassed.

Direct selling of this kind will occur more often within and between enterprises as internal transactions are perfected. New systems in procurement, engineering, development, production, maintenance, executive information systems (EIS) and especially sales and marketing are beginning to bring striking changes in the way large enterprises do business. This affects their manufacturing, distribution, sales and administration. There are fewer and fewer regional centres. Factory and warehouse automation allows businesses to close smaller plant or storage sites.

Similarly, as companies install integrated executive information systems, some managers who served principally as information conduits between top strategy-makers and those who carried out instructions are also under threat. So are some management information services (MIS) executives who have been the gatekeepers between IT vendors and inexperienced users.

Globalisation

IT is both a cause and an effect of globalisation. The ability of multinational businesses such as in financial services (banking, brokerage), manufacturing, transportation, retailing and communication, to operate successfully world-wide is a direct result of IT. Because of this, consumer IT markets are also becoming global. On the one hand, there are now universal consumer desires for amusement and knowledge. On the other hand, sellers want to broaden their sales and service channels across national boundaries but must contend with certain limitations such as transborder data restrictions. Governments too are more and more dependent on globalised IT for many of their activities, including defence, diplomacy and trade.

Convergence

Convergence is the cumulative effect of the four trends described above. Distinctions are blurring between products and services, content and media, home and business use, information and entertainment and between modes of IT such as computing and telecommunications or audio, data and video.

Companies which used to compete in a single business cluster find themselves more involved with other clusters. This affects not only the IT industry but other industries too. The high growth and return on equity of the IT industry is attracting more outsiders. They are attracted because the IT industry is booming and will continue to boom. Its largest ten firms already gross around $200 billion; the largest 100 have a sales turnover of around $500 billion. The largest 300 supply about half of the worldwide market. Many large companies are moving steadily into IT supply from other sectors (Table 5.2).

Meanwhile leading IT companies are counter-attacking other industries. Their strength is that they can provide information-based services for other sectors (Table 5.3).

Table 5.2 Outsiders moving into IT supply

Company	Native sector
American Airlines	Transport
Boeing	Aerospace
Citicorp	Banking
General Motors	Cars
Sears	Retail

Table 5.3 IT-based companies moving into other sectors

Company	Target sector
American Express (First Data Resources)	Telemarketing/direct marketing
AT&T (American Transtech)	Telemarketing/direct marketing
McDonnell Douglas Information Systems	Healthcare

Table 5.4 IT diversification failures

Company	Target sector
ITT	Communications equipment
General Electric/RCA	Computers
GTE	Securities quotation systems
Olivetti	Automated telling machines
Xerox	Computers

But diversifiers both within and outside IT should heed the lessons learned over the past five to ten years by corporations, such as Xerox and Olivetti, which have tried this route and failed (Table 5.4).

INCREASING, MERGERS AND ACQUISITIONS

One significant result of convergence is a rapidly growing tendency among IT players to strengthen affiliations with others through acquisitions, stakeholdings, joint ventures or partnerships.

Globalisation, too, frequently entails finding new affiliations and partnerships. One goal of becoming global is to gain economies of scale by spreading rising costs over a broader geographical base. Even the largest firms find it difficult to deepen their penetration into foreign markets on their own. Globalisation also helps to gain access to important new markets, technologies and skills. This is the principal reason for the recent invasion of North America by European and Asian firms, see Table 5.5.

In the software sector, acquisitions and mergers are even more numerous. Some companies are even acquiring and being acquired almost simultaneous-

Table 5.5 European IT acquisitions in the US/Canada

Company	Target sector
Alcatel	ITT's communications equipment business
British Telecom	Mitel, Canada (partial)
British Telecom	Dialcom
Logica	Data Architects
Maxwell Communications	IBM's science research institute
Reuters	Rich Inc.
Reuters	IP Sharp, Canada
Siemens	Telecom Plus

Table 5.6 Major IT acquisitions and mergers

B & C	Atlantic Computer
Burroughs	Sperry
Citicorp	Quotron
Cray	Marcol
Dowty	Case
Dun & Bradstreet	McCormack & Dodge, IMS International
Granada	DPCE
General Motors	EDS, MTech
IBM	Rolm
MCI	SBS
Plessey	Hoskyns
NYNEX	BIS Group, AGS Computers
Sema Metra	CAP Group
Systems Designers	Scicon
Unisys	Timeplex, Convergent

ly—the BIS Group, acquired by NYNEX in 1987 as part of its rapidly growing Information Solutions Group, acquired affiliations with two other information services companies, Computer Catalysts and CAP International, within a year. Convergence naturally brings together a telecommunications company such as NYNEX with an information services company such as the BIS Group, and AGS in 1989, see Table 5.6.

The value of such deals is increasing rapidly. Only a year or two ago the average cost of an acquisition was between $3 million and $5 million. Moreover three-quarters of the companies concerned were little known, privately held businesses. Now even the leading players of the software industry are regularly buying and selling.

Acquisition is just one way to diversify. More and more firms will rely on external development. For example, partnerships between manufacturers and marketing companies will become more common.

THE TRENDS DRIVE EACH OTHER

The five trends of value-added services, compatibility, direct selling, globalisation and convergence are all interrelated and mutually reinforcing. The quest for better services drives the quest for compatibility; compatibility enables direct selling; direct selling leads to globalisation and globalisation fosters convergence. And, to close the loop, convergence stimulates the IT-literacy which drives demand for value-added.

This mutual reinforcement suggests that the strategic importance of the five trends will grow exponentially for both buyers and sellers of IT goods and services. The barriers such as the lack of standards, inexperience of IT and over-regulation, are gradually being dismantled.

THE USER'S RESPONSE

So how should the user respond to all this?

Executives dealing with information and telecommunications have to ask themselves:

- How can IT help us seize sustainable product, market or operational advantages compared to our major competitors?
- What information resource management (IRM) strategies are practical in an increasingly decentralised business environment?
- What benefits in terms of cost reduction and improved productivity can IT realistically be expected to bring?
- What changes in the organisation will be necessary to achieve those benefits?
- How can we win and keep the involvement and commitment of the most senior management?
- How can we integrate IRM services and resources with the rest of the business?
- What standards should we apply to integrating systems architecture?
- What skills does a chief information officer require?

No single IRM framework can reconcile theory with reality. Different approaches will apply in different companies and even in different divisions of the same company. Many uncontrollable and sometimes conflicting factors, both internal and external, interact in a complex way. The IRM challenge is to develop a strategy in the face of this complexity.

Planning

Planning is the key. These are the crucial objectives:

- focus on critical issues in a structured manner;
- provide a framework to improve short-term and long-term investment;
- identify new opportunities;
- reduce uncertainty and risk;
- cut costs;
- improve communications;
- anticipate change;
- increase competitive advantage.

In order to convert the IRM concept into reality, top management must understand the complex pressures of the environment. The planning process must accommodate these conflicting forces if it is to achieve integration. Figure 5.2 shows some of the skills which it must harness.

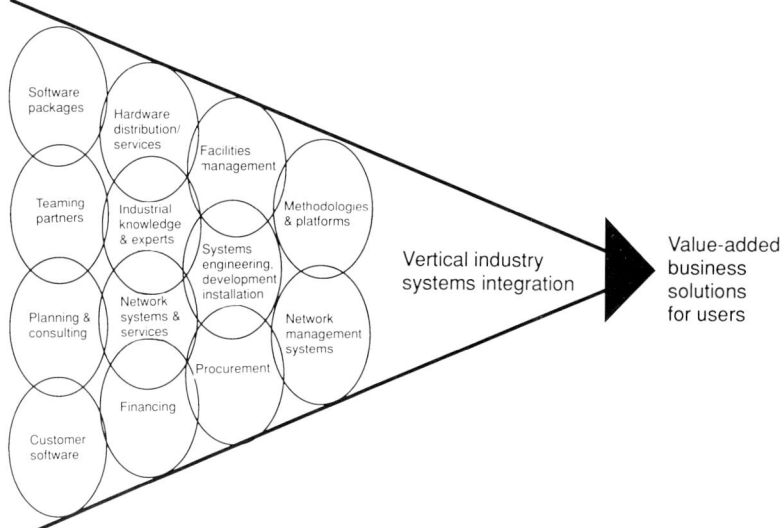

Figure 5.2   Capabilities needed to develop integrated solutions

IRM planning encompasses several phases. Each addresses a fundamental question for example:

- Where are we?
- Why should we change or not change?
- What could we do?
- What should we do?
- How do we get there?

Figure 5.3 shows how to develop such a planning process.

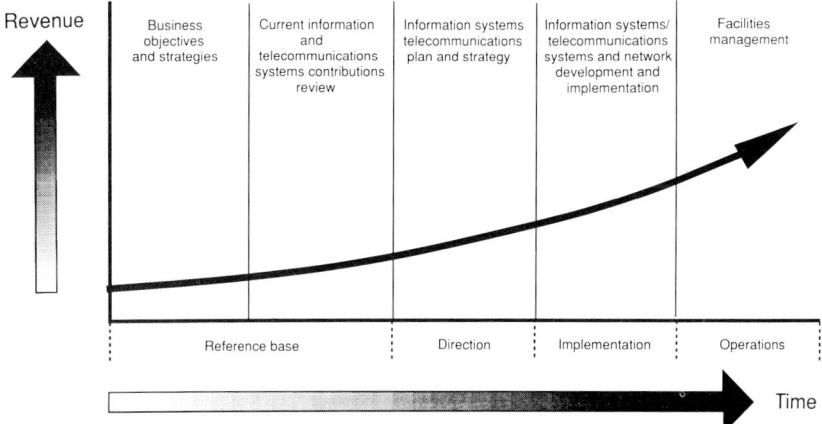

Figure 5.3   Value-added user solutions

The reference base provides an environmental profile of the internal and external factors influencing the business. It assesses problems, resources, costs, strengths, weaknesses and pressures for change. The second phase relates business issues and objectives to IRM issues and objectives. Next should come an analysis of strategic alternatives. This involves evaluating IRM alternatives in terms of organisation structure, resource requirements, advantages and disadvantages and opportunities, combining IRM and business factors.

When top management has decided upon its strategy, it needs to develop a plan that includes details of hardware, software, telecommunications, critical information and personnel. It must adopt a methodology, which will translate the plan into projects by stages – from feasibility study, through design, resource allocation, implementation, and so on.

At a corporate level, it must aim to introduce a common data dictionary, standards for corporate-wide systems, consolidated financial systems, other common systems, company-wide networks, common databases, applications packages, data elements and common protocols. At the same time, top management must ensure continuity of the services that support the business. Information systems, security, disaster prevention and recovery plans all fall into this domain. Many companies have neglected this area and failed to educate their people on the subject.

In planning for greater productivity and measuring progress towards it, it is necessary to take into account not only 'hard cash' factors such as salaries and benefits, office space, inventory and equipment, office overheads (lighting, heating, mail, phones), external services and travel, but also less easily quantified factors such as time savings, improved processes, higher throughput, better customer service and better company image.

The role of the chief information officer

The chief information officer (CIO) is responsible for planning and co-ordinating the direction of these IRM investments. Though many of the operational responsibilities are decentralised, it makes sense to have functions such as strategic planning, standards, corporate systems and networks integration guided by a centralised group.*

Among his objectives should be:

- to get away from 'firefighting' exercises;
- to build a multi-disciplinary staff;
- to separate strategy from operations;
- to integrate telecommunications, information systems and business plans:

---

* See Dr Gad J. Selig's *Strategic Planning for Information Resource Management in a Multinational Environment*, UMI Research Press, Ann Arbor, Michigan, 1983.

- to get practical action under way, while avoiding internal politics and being overwhelmed by vendors and their technology.

A clear IRM framework should help business and IRM managers establish a planning environment, which will support the running of the business.

The key success factors will be:

- winning support from the top (executive sponsorship);
- establishing a CIO;
- involving people at every level;
- having a clear planning process;
- applying project management disciplines;
- asking the right fundamental questions;
- establishing the corporate role;
- tracking costs and benefits.
- implement the plan.

Start small and complete the process. Be flexible, for change is inevitable.

6

THE CONVERGENCE OF
COMPUTERS AND
TELECOMMUNICATIONS

'Telecommunications networks and computer systems are developing rapidly. As both acquire increasing flexibility and intelligence, both rely for future development on each other. In such an environment, the two industries are bound to converge', says Casimir Skrzypczak, Vice President, Science and Technology, NYNEX Corporation.

Twenty years ago computing was focused on centralised mainframes which were primarily engaged in batch processing, while the telecommunications industry was almost exclusively voice-based. The computer industry was the spawning ground for many new firms, while the telephone industry was dominated by national monopolies, such as the US's Bell System. Things have changed radically since then. Workers now interact directly with computers at their desktops, phone lines carry an ever-growing volume of data, computer firms are in communications, the unified Bell System has been dismembered and a growing number of telecommunication firms worldwide are providing computer services.

Looking ahead over the next twenty years, it is clear that there will be continued dramatic advances in the interconnectivity and integration of computers and their communications channels.

THE HISTORICAL PERSPECTIVE IN
TELECOMMUNICATIONS

In the 1960s a number of technological innovations made a significant impact on the transmission of voice and data information. The first was direct dialling of long distance calls which had spread by the mid-1960s to include more than 90 per cent of the US Bell System customers.

Then in 1965, the first electronic switching system, the No 1 ESS, was installed in the United States. This central office switch differed from its electromechanical predecessors because it used electronics and a stored program, (i.e. a computer) for control. Stored program control made it possible to add vertical features and automate many operator functions. A heavy reliance was placed on communication standards for complete, interoperative ability between switches. The 1 ESS was replaced later in the 1960s by the 1 AESS and many systems of this design still remain in service. These switches, with their greater capacity and functionality, are at the heart of many of the improvements in communications networks today.

Around the same time as the introduction of the electronic switches, telecommunication companies began to develop private, intelligent, analogue PBX equipment. These PBXs resided on the premises of businesses and controlled their own internal phone system. In effect, these intelligent PBXs were also computers and they provided additional features not available on the public network.

In the early 1970s, the business demand for data communications began to take off. Previously, data could only be transferred at 1200bps over voice circuits and then only with special line conditioning. By 1970 high speed data communications had increased to 4800bps and was still increasing in speed. Higher speed communications were augmented by advances in signalling processing. Value-added data networks started to emerge alongside the basic voice transport communications networks, to support communications between business computer terminals.

Signalling is the communication between switching offices. In 1976, an out-of-band signalling system network known as common channel inter-office signalling (CCIS) became operational. This was the largest packet switching system network in the world. It speeded up voice call set-up, could transmit signals in both directions at once and improved the efficiency and management of the networks. This was the first major use of data communications to assist in voice communications operation.

'Digital' electronics provided greater transmission speed with fewer errors than in analogue transmissions for both voice and data transmissions. Though end-to-end digital service (ie. on all parts of the line) was limited primarily to within or between large urban areas by the late 1970s, plans were made in the United States for nationwide interconnection by the early 1990s.

By the 1980s the need for communication capacity, functionality and services had increased dramatically. Monopolies were a thing of the past. Deregulation of the PTTs in the US, UK, Japan, Netherlands and West Germany began. This deregulation greatly increased competition. The increase in competition and the greater dependency on technology by virtually all facets of society speeded up the introduction of products and services to end-users.

THE PRESENT PERSPECTIVE IN TELECOMMUNICATIONS

Under today's network architecture (shown in Figure 6.1), individual customers are connected through a central office switch. The phone number is permanently associated with that customer's physical location. So today's network intelligence is nodal, i.e. related to a specific point, a local or central office switch. The range of features that may be offered to the customer is usually limited to those that are provided by the central office switch hardware manufacturer. The development cycle for making significant new features available to customers can be as long as five years.

Today, public communication networks are relying more and more on optical fibre, which has far greater capacity and reliability than copper wires. In addition to trunk lines, fibre is also being used in place of cable in crowded conduit paths under roads, in metropolitan areas and inside buildings.

Communication hardware has gradually developed far greater intelligence. Modems, multiplexors, concentrators and other equipment are all capable of carrying out some network management activities. The operations and support systems that administer and maintain the public voice networks are sophisticated networked computer processors.

PBXs are now highly intelligent, digitally-based computers. Among their functions are the ability to automatically distribute calls to operators, to perform least-cost routing of the telephone calls, to provide voice-coded responses to special prompts and to support local area data networks.

Data communication has also improved greatly. Underwater cable and fibre and satellites proliferate, and currently provide some 56-kilobits/second (kbps)

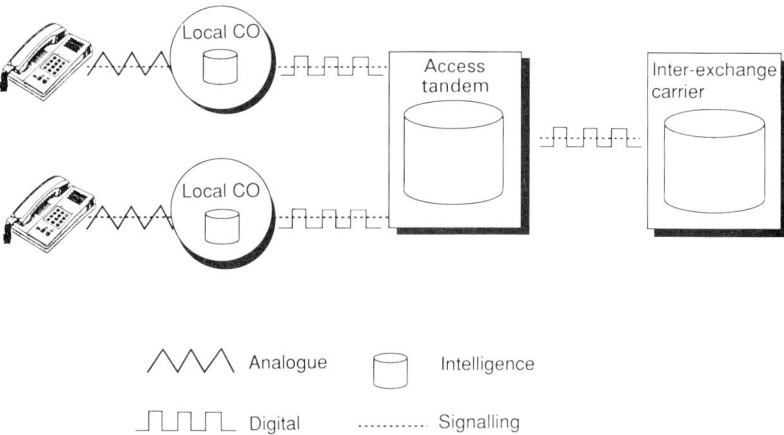

Figure 6.1   Current communications network architecture

of data interconnection between emerging communication networks in North America, Europe and the Far East. There is a much greater demand for and availability of wideband 1.5Mbps and higher.

Whereas the 1980s was originally considered the decade of the local area network (LAN), today's emphasis has shifted to include the metropolitan area network (MAN), too. More and more broadband (1.5 to 10Mbps) networks are being installed to support the greater demand for higher transmission speeds for graphics and images. Where cable was used to support LAN terminal connections, existing voice twisted pair wiring is now frequently used to support both voice and data computer connections.

Looking at the recent history and present state of communications, it is clear that electronics and computer hardware and software have been the driving forces behind the increased speed, capacity and functionality of telecommunication networks.

THE FUTURE PERSPECTIVE IN TELECOMMUNICATIONS

So how will telecommunications evolve in the future? Telecommunication companies are moving toward developing a 'universal intelligent network': one that

- knows about people rather than just phone numbers:
- allows users easily to obtain flexible, customised services;
- provides multi-media connections to users;
- enables all calls to be completed through the use of various voice storage and retrieval services.

The intelligent network will use the flexibility of information processing to create customised services for individual large customers or for groups of smaller subscribers. Software and the ability to create new software are the basis for the introduction of these services.

This network architecture may evolve in a number of ways. Its full implementation adds shared programmable intelligence (see below) to provide new service, on the existing switching network. The local offices and inter-exchange carriers continue to provide transport capabilities through existing switches and relay tandems. A parallel packet switching network provides signalling access to the intelligence. The common service intelligence is provided through distributed general computers with databases, as shown in Figure 6.2. These computers add capabilities and flexibility. They can be programmed to provide a wide range of services, customised for individual

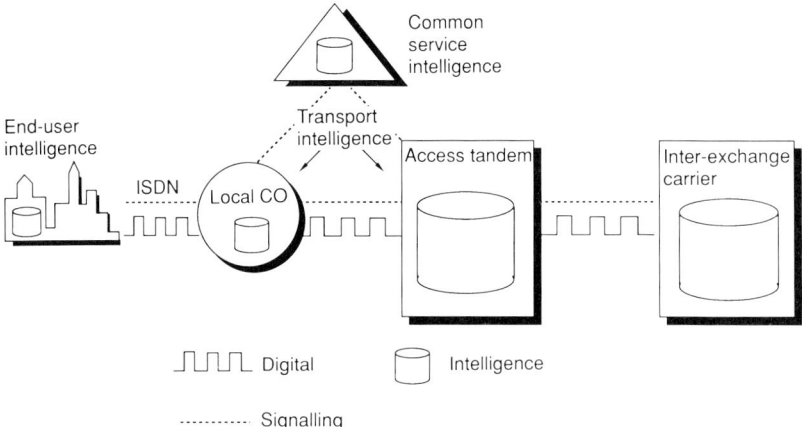

Figure 6.2   Future communications network architecture

subscribers. As central office switches evolve, some of these features will be incorporated into the hardware itself.

An example of an intelligent network application is the personal telephone number concept. Here a telephone number is associated with the individual subscriber, rather than with a telephone line and instrument. As the individual moves around, he or she can notify the system where to route calls. Callers will not have to remember more than one number for an individual. Furthermore, users can each have their own profile of services associated with their number. These may include speed calling, distinctive ringing, automatic recall, pre-announcement and selective call rejection.

Another example is the 'virtual private network'. Working with private PBXs, the public intelligent switches now permit the development of worldwide, private data and voice business networks using shared public facilities. Here customers will be able to maintain the control and management previously available in private networks, while at the same time benefiting from the reduced costs and improved security associated with the public network.

The evolution in telecommunications is away from nodal intelligence and towards distributed common service databases. Intelligence is no longer specific or hardwired to a particular point in the network, but is now held in a database common to many switches. These databases will become the vehicle through which networks of processors share information, while processors manipulate the data in many ways. Information services will build naturally from these concepts. As this happens, transport networks will increasingly become a commodity. The real value-added will come from networks that provide broad communications, unifying telephone, data, image and video communications. An increasing demand for higher bandwidth to allow faster data communication transfer already reflects this evolution. Businesses need a

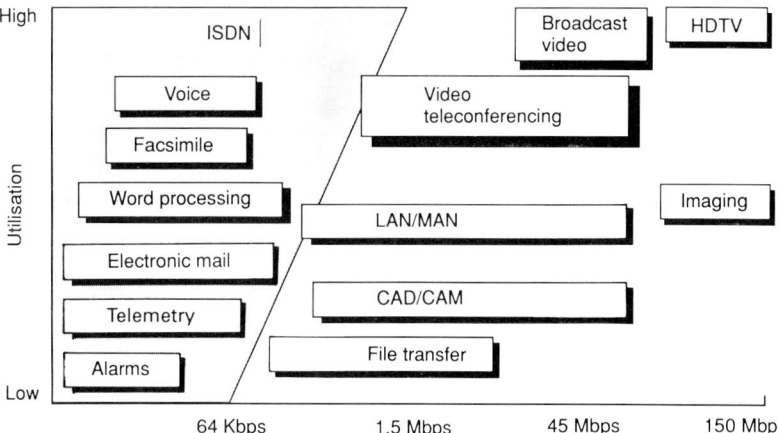

Figure 6.3   The diverse transmission capacity requirements of various applications

minimum of 1.5Mbps now, and demand is growing for 45Mbps. 'H4', a channel rate of 140Mbps, appears certain to become a future standard. The diverse transmission capacity requirement of various applications is given in Figure 6.3.

Many value-added information services can only be provided over a broadband network. The wideband networks of 1.5Mbps or higher that are evolving rapidly now will provide integrated access to a variety of high speed digital communicating media. Various telematic services will transmit voice, text, data, photographs, drawings and other materials. In doing so, they will displace much present movement of paper and magnetic media. Simultaneous use of multiple media will be essential for communication among people who have a need to share materials just as they do in face-to-face meetings. Searching, filtering, composing, transforming, editing and interpreting information will be simplified and enhanced.

The intelligence behind this broadband network, that was a dream just a few years ago, is becoming a reality. It is no longer a matter of whether – just when. Only the dates are left to be filled in as technical, regulatory and economic questions are resolved one by one.

The private data networks and the public networks will battle to capture the market by developing new cost-effective value-added services and products. The outcome of this battle will be determined by the ability to most effectively apply new technology in response to customer needs. New products must reach the market quickly and be targetted to consumers who have no previous technical experience. Most probably, businesses and end-users will use combinations of services from public and private value-added networks.

THE HISTORICAL PERSPECTIVE IN COMPUTING

Computers began as stand-alone, central processors performing batch functions. The 1960s began the development of online transaction processing with multiple dumb terminals in the same location. The 1970s allowed users to access remote terminals (see Figure 6.4). This necessitated the development of data communication protocols. Their only standards were proprietary standards set by computer vendors for their own hardware and software.

As the cost of processing dropped, centralised processing evolved to include departmental processing minis. These tended to employ a new architecture that was largely incompatible with (and hence unable to communicate with) centralised mainframes. Data communication protocols evolved rapidly, becoming faster and more reliable.

The 1980s started the development of large computer data networks that spanned numerous business locations. These data networks tended to be hierarchical in nature. The central mainframe controlled the departmental minis and the departmental minis controlled the terminals. Terminals could not talk to each other and rarely could minis talk to each other.

An ever-increasing percentage of computer processing was employed in the management of network facilities and functions. IBM's approach to medium to large SNA (System Network Architecture) networks was to establish a separate mini or mainframe totally dedicated to enabling computers to talk to each other and to manage networks. Two of the biggest challenges were the merging of dissimilar data networks and the ability to monitor and maintain diverse computer and communications equipment.

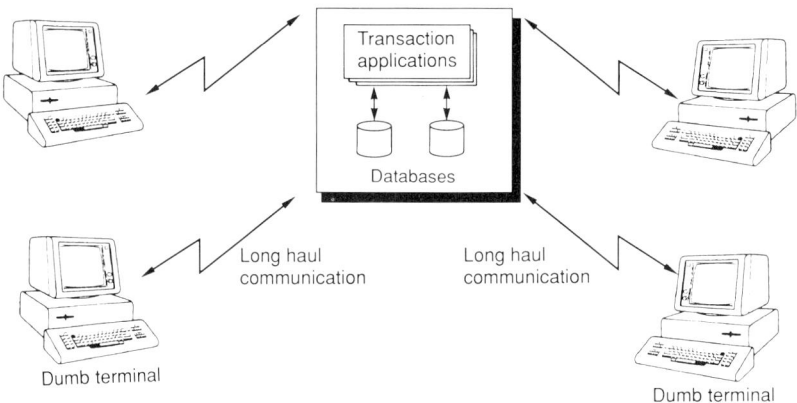

Figure 6.4   Traditional centralised computer processing

In the 1980s the personal computer brought processing closer to the end-users. For the first time they did not have to rely on remote computer processing facilities, which were often slow and liable to communication failure.

THE CURRENT PERSPECTIVE OF COMPUTING

The last 20 years have brought a dramatic expansion of computer communications. Our old ideas have been outstripped by the new needs for computer communications. The driving forces for these communication capabilities are computerised businesses with globalised day-to-day operations. These expanded computer communications use the communications channel for transport and signalling, and support the integrity of end-user software applications.

The demand for computer processing power linked by communications is growing steadily. This will be made easier by the increasing power of computers. It is expected that the cost per MIP (million instructions per second) will fall below $1000 in smaller machines in less than two years. It is also the stated aim of IBM to have the power of one of its largest machines on the desktop by the early 1990s.

Today, at all levels of processing, computers are becoming communicating processors. In the early 1970s distributed data processing failed to catch on because computers were so diverse and because there were no effective strategies for linking them. Today distributed processing not only allows computers in two locations to access each other's data and to split processing, but also allows remote applications to work on a co-operative basis. Hence the new term 'co-operative processing' is often used along with 'distributed processing'. The two terms imply an ability to communicate and share data, power and functionality across multiple remote computer resources. We now see the beginnings of true peer to peer communications (Figure 6.5). The computer hierarchy will disappear as all computers communicate with each other equally rather then through a central mainframe.

Micro technology now makes it possible to have much larger programs available at a user's fingertips. He can tackle larger problems and customise software for his own needs more easily on his personal computer. A particularly important recent development is the linking of personal computers and distributed processors through local and metropolitan area networks with file servers and distributed databases. This enables users to share programs, data bases and resources such as printers.

To sum up these developments, the evolution of computing requires increased processing speed and improvements in distributed processing. Both

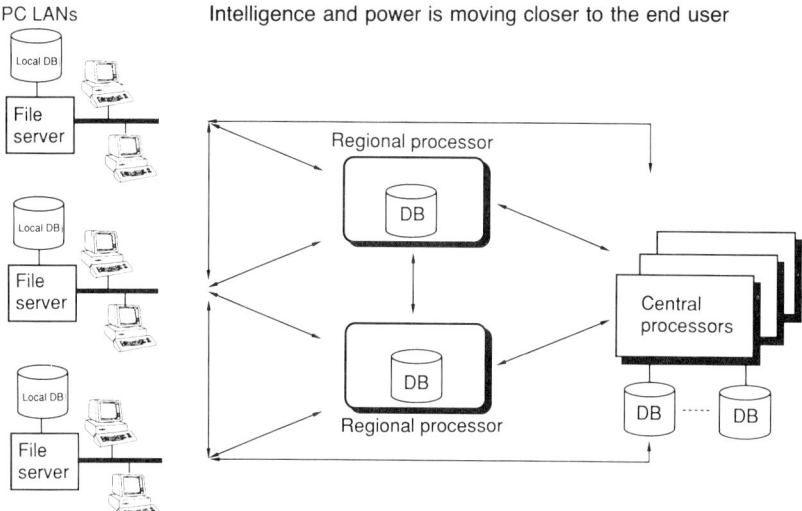

Figure 6.5   Peer to peer distributed processing

of these trends demand highly distributed, fully interconnected digital communications facilities, which operate at a high transfer rate.

THE FUTURE PERSPECTIVE OF COMPUTING

The computer industry will continue to experience rapid technological advance. Computers and computer networking will proliferate. Two elements will lead to this growth. Firstly, more and more computers used for multiple applications across all industries, will need to communicate between each other. Secondly, new and innovative technologies will make computers attractive to the less sophisticated, less trained end-user.

Computer processors will appear in more and more applications. For example, they will become integral to manufacturing as robotics grows. In the home, built-in control processors will regulate doors, lights, microwave ovens and television sets. Many homes will have communication screens in several rooms and will use them to obtain entertainment and information such as electronic newspapers and video rentals directly through data feeds. We expect a greater variety of computer-based, hand-held devices that use radio for local commmunications. One early example of this is Avis's use of a portable terminal for checking return car rentals. Another is the use of smart cards for payment of road tolls and parking meters.

There will be greater and greater communications between central processing units. Human intervention will be limited as industries become ever more dependent on computers for basic information services. Several areas such as electronic trading will show high growth. Computers already handle repetitive trades and schedule events to assist traders on a 24-hour basis.

The establishment of a global marketplace will arise in part through electronic data interchange (EDI) for electronic purchasing. In order to compete with US suppliers, Japan and South Korea are proposing implementations of EDI in the automobile industry between themselves and the US. For computers to become truly communicating processors, a universal communications language will be necessary. This will be greatly assisted by the development of EDIFACT, a universal trading dictionary.

Most developed countries will make increased use of electronic funds transfer (EFT) for paying business invoices. People will use debit cards or smart cards for personal expenditures such as automatic bill payments and store shopping. (Debit cards cause computer to computer transactions to be switched through financial networks to debit a customer's account directly and credit the merchant's account). Business and personal use of EFT could pave the way for a cashless society and eventually a universal monetary system.

The end-user's supermicro will increase in power and online capability. Mainframes and minis will evolve to become repositories of databases, controlling communicating sessions and offline functions such as billing and archiving.

Computer techniques to display information will be more encompassing in scope. Screens with 100 Mbit resolution will allow more detailed images. Through computer networks, end users will interact on an increasingly interpersonal basis.

Distributed PC/supermicros will be interconnected in local, metro and wide

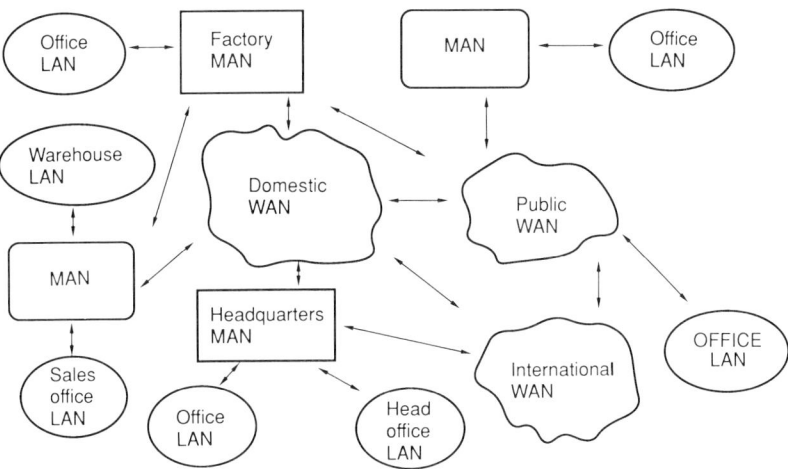

Figure 6.6   Local, metro and wide area networking

area networks, often on an international basis, both within and between enterprises. A buyer in the US and an architect of another company in Italy may simultaneously display and edit an image of a 35mm photograph, while discussing the image and the changes they are making.

Because of the increased importance of networks, each maker's equipment will have to be able to talk to any other. This equipment will eventually be configured into multiple data networks instead of separate networks with access to other networks through gateways. Each multiple computer data network in turn will be considered as a unit. The challenge will be to inter-network them (see Figure 6.6) in a way that allows cross communication in realtime.

TELECOMMUNICATIONS IN SUPPORT OF COMPUTER APPLICATIONS

The highly distributed, fully interconnected digital communications facilities, operating at high data rates, will only be possible on a person-to-person basis with the evolution of a 'public' data network capability, along the same lines as the public voice network with IDDD (international direct distance dialling). With this data network anyone will be able to reach and send information to anyone else at business and home or through the use of publicly available voice/data/graphics terminals. An indication of the expected growth in this area is given in Figure 6.7.

The illustration only shows the increase by 2400bps modems in data transmissions, which will increase by at least 20 per cent compounded annually for the next 10 years. If we include other modem speeds and expand the local

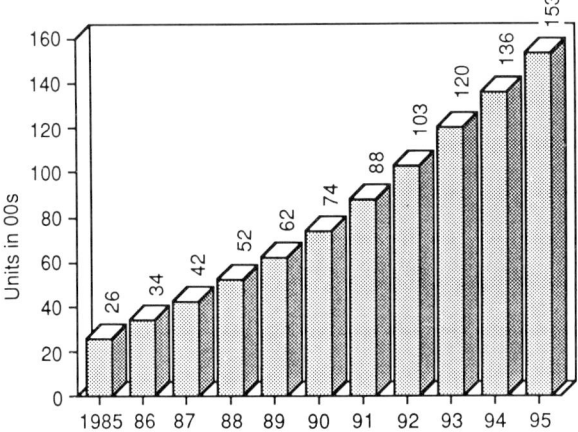

Figure 6.7 Statistical projection of increase in data traffic over the US public voice network. Forecast in the use of 2400 bps modems across all industries as proxy for protecting the increase of data transmission over voice lines

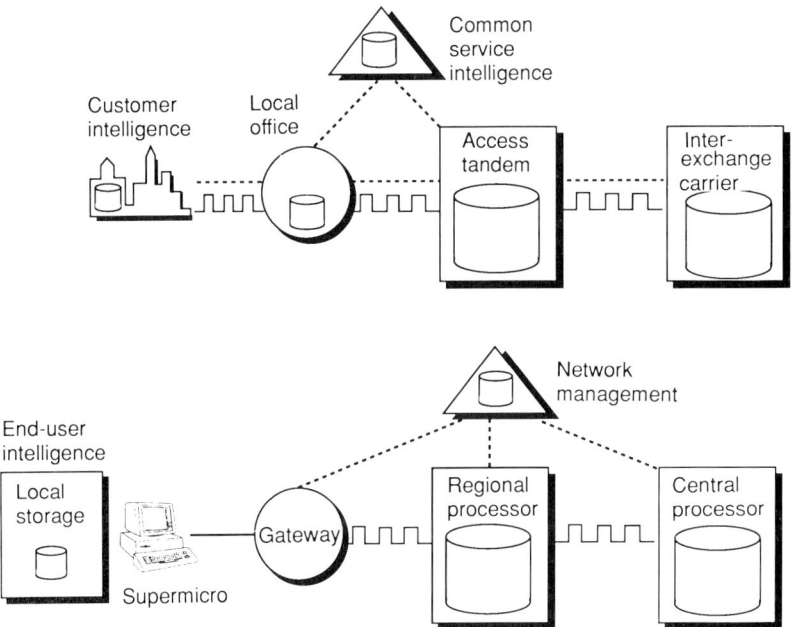

Figure 6.8 Similarity between computer and communications networks. There is the issue of intelligence in the user's device versus the network

loop to support text, video and image, the increase in traffic and the potential revenue opportunities for networks will be significantly larger.

Today end-users are unaware of the architecture, switches, processors and links that comprise the public voice network. This will also be true of computer networks. Originally a corporation had one intelligent computer centre; this then grew to several centres. Ultimately it will be viewed as one 'enterprise computer' and one 'enterprise database'. End-users will be unaware of the local, regional and networked central computers and databases.

The issue of the day is the quantity of intelligence in the computer terminal versus that in the network. There must be co-operation between the end-user terminal equipment and the network enhancements if there is to be effective interconnectivity. Computers will function best if they take advantage of the network resources and capabilities. In the past we had dumb terminals with intelligent users. In the future we will need intelligent terminals that can interact with the less sophisticated user. We also need intelligent networks to provide enhanced broadband capabilities. Not only will end-user computers need to talk computer communication protocols, they will also need to speak a complex network language.

This is particularly true of ISDN (integrated services digital network). ISDN provides a single conduit to a variety of services, such as voice, data, image and facsimile. In the past, if a voice circuit was busy, only a human could tell, not the telephone. Now with multiple network services user equipment will need to track the state of the shared link. Similarly the network will need the intelligence to understand the attributes of user equipment, if it is to handle the bandwidth speed and information transfers correctly. The intelligence of the communication network central office needs to be matched by the intelligence of the equipment on customer premises. This implies a critical need for standards.

THE PROBLEM OF STANDARDS

Standards present one area of potential divergence between computers and communications. Traditionally, communication networks relied heavily on standards because individual switches and terminals had to be compatible. Now communication companies are expanding their transport networks with intelligent, value-added services based on their own or interim standards. This relaxing of standards largely brought on by competitive forces could potentially limit exchanges between the networks and between international communications companies.

At the same time, the computer companies originally developed proprietary standards for their own equipment. Now, with growing pressure from customers, they are being forced to agree among themselves to allow greater interaction.

International standards such as those developed through the International Standards Organisation (ISO), primarily support computer communications. Unfortunately there is no clear division in the seven-layer ISO model between communication equipment functions and computer equipment functions. So development of effective standards between computers and telecommunication utilities is still in its infancy. This will have an impact on the matching of intelligence in user equipment and in the network.

The competitive situation also has some influence on the pace of standardisation. The 1970s and early 1980s witnessed the early salvos in the battle of the giants, IBM and AT&T, in the US. (This was prompted by the 'Carterphone' decision, which allowed vendors other than communication utilities to attach equipment to communication circuits.) IBM moved into the communications business with shares in a common carrier and the purchase of a PBX company; AT&T started to produce computers. Fifteen years later each seem to be backing off. IBM is selling off its stock in MCI microwave communications and AT&T 3B computers are still struggling to establish themselves.

The battleground is changing. The computer industry is establishing niches for itself and providing pieces of the pie, primarily software; the communications companies on the other hand are becoming more service-oriented, emphasising the integration of products and services. Computer vendors can provide their own networks. Communciation vendors can provide intelligence in their networks. Because each industry has the capability for the other's technology, the impetus to develop strong standards and to develop matched intelligence co-operatively has had only limited success.

With the battleground wide open, this forces the entry of a third party–the business user. If computer and communication industries cannot agree, business needs and alliances will force both sides to accept the concept of the open network architecture for standard interoperability. This will bring about the ultimate convergence of computers and telecommunications.

THE KEY IS NEW SERVICES–INFORMATION AND ERGONOMICS

Convergence will bring many opportunities for new services and products for end-users. The level and range of services that these industries will provide will be largely determined by two emerging key technologies shared by computers and telecommunications, as shown in Figure 6.9–informatics and ergonomics.

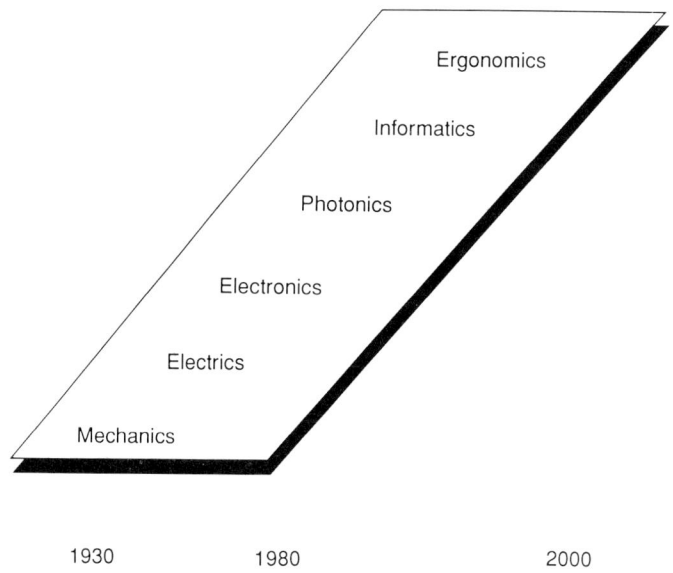

Ergonomics

Informatics

Photonics

Electronics

Electrics

Mechanics

1930   1980   2000

Figure 6.9   The critical path of technological evolution

Informatics

In this context informatics means the ability to produce software in an economic and timely fashion so that the advance in electronics and photonics can be fully exploited. The computer industry is notorious for its three–five year backlog in developing applications. Software development needs to be greatly improved, for example, through artificial intelligence, fifth generation and natural language development, auto code generation and re-useable, building-block software. The ability of the public network to provide flexible, customised services required by the future telecommunications user will depend on the rate of progress that can be made in informatics. Network planners and implementers will have to learn to transfer these capabilties to the public network as it evolves to the intelligent network.

Ergonomics

This is the design of computer interfaces that meet the personal needs of the individual, providing easy, effective interaction. Informatics may well result in new information services that the mass market may want and need. But those services will not gain acceptance if users are not willing, say, to learn a new computer language. People require interfaces, which allow them to communicate with machines, networks and other people (see Figure 6.10), using the natural human senses and language. These include enabling technologies such as speech recognition, machine vision, natural languages and machine intelligence. Unless we achieve major breakthroughs in ergonomics, the problem that many potential users of a service find it too difficult to either learn or remember how to use, will become even more acute. Which of us knows how to use more than three or four of the dozens of functions available with the modern telephone system? Interactions need to be simple and intuitive. This is particularly true of the public network, which numbers among its strongest assets the ability to offer products to the entire population.

CONCLUSION

With increasing reliance on computers and networks to perform everyday, personal and business functions, computers and networks will have to be much more sophisticated, reliable and maintainable in the coming decades. This means that a great deal of effort will have to go into assuring that the networks are reliable, secure, easily reconfigurable and under total control. Most present network management offerings focus on limited elements of the networks. In

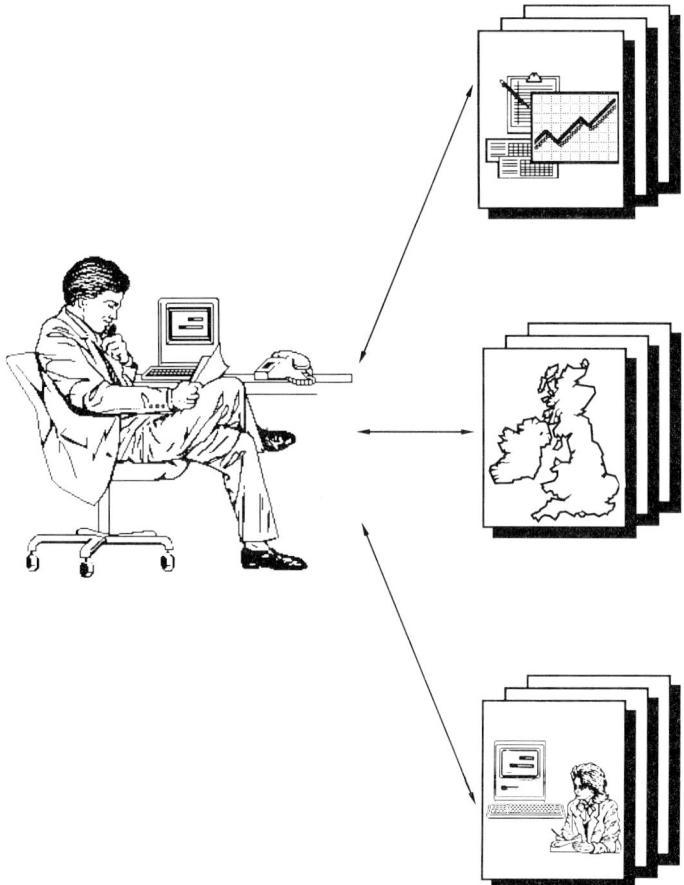

Figure 6.10   End-user interface

future, networks will be controlled by a 'manager of managers' which will exert the unifying force for effective operation and interaction of data, voice and computer networks.

This task will not be easy. Networks are highly complex, have many elements, come from multiple vendors and are interconnected over a wide variety of loosely coupled telecommunications systems. They interface with both PTTs and independent carriers, and with multiplexors, concentrators, switches and computers from different vendors.

Tomorrow's converged information markets will emphasise service systems that have a short production cycle, are dynamic and have a short lifetime. The markets will reward companies that sell building-blocks, and which can quickly program or code them into new or improved products and services.

Our government leaders will have to create an environment that does not impose arbitrary limitations on how far or how rapidly companies can implement intelligent communication network technology. The computer vendors cannot be entirely responsible for new information services. They will need to work with the communication industry as partners.

The companies that will claim a lion's share in the information services industry will be those who are most responsive to the end-user. If the provider of services capitalises on what the user wants today. Even though it will probably change tomorrow, demand will soon outstrip supply. That in turn, will hasten the inevitable convergence of computers and telecommunications.

7

FINANCIAL FUTURES: THE MANAGEMENT OF DISCONTINUITY

'The financial services industry is in the midst of rapid and dramatic upheaval. Six major trends will dominate the future of the industry in the coming decades, and will decide who the global and local winners are' says Rob Wood, Marketing and Planning Manager of The BIS Group.

Remember the bank on the corner? The one with the big wood-panelled doors, lots of brass knobs, high counters, marble floors and rows of tellers counting out freshly minted notes behind large bars? And the bank manager, who occasionally wrote to you to tell you that you were overdrawn or who advised you on great occasions such as the drawing of a will, on the investment of spare cash or on your small business? What did that bank do for you? It kept your money and precious assets safe, cleared your cheques, occasionally lent you money and managed some of your savings.

There is now an amazing proliferation of other organisations which do things with your money; building societies, stockbrokers, insurance brokers, life and general insurance companies, futures/options brokers and dealers, merchant banks, factoring agencies, confirming houses, bond/gilts dealers and market makers and so on.

These organisations may not appear to have much in common, but the functions which they perform overlap. As shown in this diagram (Figure 7.1) those functions are sixfold. The infrastructure of the financial services sector consists of four groups of systems which intersect with particular functions of the sector at specific points, known as the front and back offices:

Now let us switch to a shot of a bank in the year 2000. At first glance it looks just like any other modern building of the 21st century: glass and alloy exterior, interior walls lined with video displays – an ergonomic office, designed around small groups of people. What we notice as we stand in the foyer is that most of the customers are 'interfacing' with video displays inside transparent acoustic domes. The reason why the bank has so few people in it is that most clients deal with it through their home terminals, though the occasional visit may still be necessary to draw cash or actually see someone. The most interesting thing we

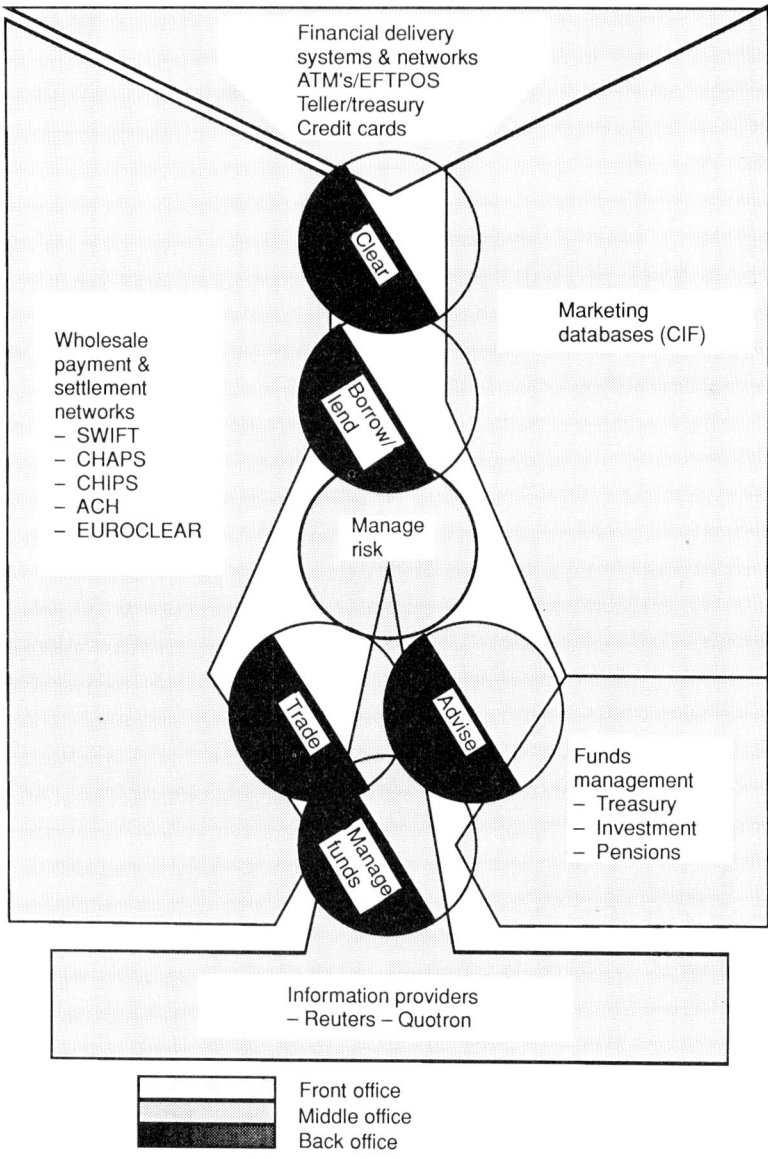

Financial delivery
systems & networks
ATM's/EFTPOS
Teller/treasury
Credit cards

Marketing
databases (CIF)

Wholesale
payment &
settlement
networks
– SWIFT
– CHAPS
– CHIPS
– ACH
– EUROCLEAR

Clear

Borrow/
lend

Manage
risk

Trade

Advise

Manage
funds

Funds
management
– Treasury
– Investment
– Pensions

Information providers
– Reuters – Quotron

Front office
Middle office
Back office

Figure 7.1   Functional model of financial services

notice is the absence of paper. All the staff use small terminals, hand-held or
built into their workstations. The bank is not doing anything very different to
what it used to do for your father or grandfather; it is just doing it in a totally
different way. Current accounts still exist, but savings accounts have now been
replaced by several varieties of demand deposit accounts. Cheque books and
credit cards have largely been replaced by a single card, the debit card. You can

buy shares, bonds and insurance through your home terminal or the branch video interface.

Information technology will have transformed the relationship between large corporations and their bankers. Electronic data interchange has resulted in two types of corporate clients for banks: those who rely on the bank to do certain accounting and cash control functions for them (usually the smaller companies) and larger clients who are so sophisticated in managing their treasury that they simply ask the bank to download their financial information daily and do the rest themselves.

Most large corporations are self-sufficient in raising money in the domestic and international equity, bond and money markets, and in trading in the secondary markets in their own and other companies paper. They also handle their own foreign exchange trading. The smaller companies will communicate with their banker through large, tablet-type terminals (like the ubiquitous videophones, except with a bigger touch pad), initiating transactions and accessing the treasury management information provided to them by the bank.

The vast floors of dealing rooms and stock exchanges, built in the years of helter-skelter growth in the 1970s and 1980s by major market makers and stock and futures/options exchanges, will be deserted, or converted into pleasuredomes and health clubs. The blood coursing through the veins of the world's major financial markets will be virtually invisible. The only sign of their existence will be computer sites located in the depths of the countryside, outside major cities around the world.

Analysts, brokers and salespersons will have been decimated in numbers. Artificially intelligent software now makes portfolio decisions and buys and sells financial instruments globally, through a network of non-stop computer trading exchanges. Computer-literate market experts will fine-tune these systems to reflect their views of the market.

This is not as far-fetched a scenario as may be thought. Wells Fargo Bank has been running a successful $40 billion global equities portfolio completely by computer for a number of years.

As the number of sites of expert system-based dealing systems in the world grows from the low hundreds to the thousands, so the knowledge of financial experts will increasingly be incorporated in software. Artificial intelligence will also be applied to the routing of transactions around the world, so that transactions are carried out in the most effective manner, with the minimum number of parties involved. Both front-office and back-office costs will be cut dramatically as a result.

By the year 2000 you will have a plastic card similar to a credit card in your wallet or purse, called a smart card. This smart card will contain your bank balance, your credit card balance, some personal details and perhaps even your passport and identification details. It will be programmed so that you can draw cash, pay for all your purchases (credit or cash) in the shops, enter your office building, perhaps open the electronic lock on your car door and pay for transatlantic telephone calls from a payphone. You won't need coins, car keys or all those silly pieces of plastic, which now distort the fine lines of your wallet.

Checking through immigration on an overseas trip will be even easier – smart cards will spot terrorists and football thugs much better than immigration and security officers, so your entry to a new country will be easier than drawing cash from the automated teller machine, with no humans to hassle you.

At home, you will pay your bills, reconcile your bank statements and transfer money into your preferred investment portfolio from the comfort of your armchair at your personal computer. The telephone directory, *Yellow Pages*, and your local shopping catalogues will all be available at the press of a button, and you may be able to order some of the merchandise on screen. This is not science fiction: several pilot schemes are already testing all of these ideas in the US and Europe. The technology is available: it only remains for it to be cheap and reliable enough to be widely used.

In business almost all routine transactions with the bank, insurance company and financial advisors and brokers will be conducted via a terminal. The cost of a product or service for a financial services organisation drops by an average of 80 per cent when it is delivered through information technology rather than by a human being.

Much the same equation applies to the costs to businesses on the other side of the technology. Financial news and prices, treasury management services, insurance quotations, trade finance products and stock market and other investment products and services are already being delivered daily or in real time to businesses around the world in this way. It benefits everyone to use as much information technology as possible in financial services, even though the start-up costs may seem prohibitive.

DEVELOPING THE TECHNOLOGY

How will the financial services industry arrive at this Brave New World? Six trends dominate the future of the industry:

- Globalisation
- Changing regulatory environments
- Implementation of advanced technologies
- Changing organisational cultures
- Demographic changes in the First World
- The shifting balance of power

Globalisation

Global trade is essential to global growth. As mankind has become more and more specialised, so nations have themselves become specialists. In turn, specialisation has made us all interdependent. Information technology helps us to manage this, because it is the first technology to emerge which is built on organisation rather than specialisation. It does not force us to break the world up into ever smaller pieces, but allows us to build up a bigger picture of the world than we could otherwise do. It allows us to integrate what we know about the world, and in making sense of it, to organise our world.

The global nature of this technology is being felt most keenly in the financial services industry, where it addresses a cross-section of individual and corporate financial needs around the world.

Since the 1960s, the spread of American and Japanese multinational corporations around the world has meant that banks serving these corporations have had to provide services to their clients in all major countries around the globe.

The increasing complexity and diversity of large corporations has also resulted in a much greater demand for sophisticated and integrated banking products which address the needs of the large, global corporation. The emergence of electronic banking, Swaps and Eurofinance are good examples of this trend, driven by client demand and major financial institutions.

Changing regulatory environments

Deregulation in Europe, the US and the Pacific Rim will result in massive consolidation of the industry and a reduction in the number of players. In the UK, the Financial Services Act is probably the most advanced piece of financial services regulation in the world. Although many financial institutions have complained about certain sections of this Act, there is no doubt that it balances the need to form a level playing field for competitors, against the need to protect the interests of the unsophisticated borrower, depositor, investor or insured party.

It reflects the integrated nature of the financial services industry in the UK, where a wide variety of products and services is marketed through a single channel (such as the branch networks of the leading UK clearers). Although it brings regulation to new areas, for example, areas of the unit trust, unlisted securities and futures and option broking markets, it provides all participants in the market with a degree of certainty in their dealings, which should boost the attractiveness of the UK as a global financial centre.

In the US, penetration of the money centre banks into the interstate banking markets through Edge Act subsidiaries continues. There is a real possibility that US bank affiliates will win the right to underwrite and trade in securities, although they may be barred from engaging in real estate brokerage or development. True deregulation of the US market will not occur, however, until full competition is allowed in the interstate banking markets.

The most significant deregulation in the next few years will be in Europe. The European Community's 1992 initiative is about to have an enormous impact on both the banking and insurance sectors. Exchange controls in most EEC countries should be removed by 1992. Financial institutions will not have to apply for a licence to compete in another European country, provided they are licensed to operate by the regulatory authority in their country of origin.

Consolidation of the industry is likely to occur in Europe within the next four years as a result of these changes. This will bring lower prices, better service and simpler cross-border financial transactions. The European Currency Unit may come to replace national currencies sooner than expected, with the establishment of a European Central Bank.

Japanese financial markets have been liberalised, if not deregulated, and many foreign institutions are now able to operate in Japan subject to certain restrictions. Further liberalisation and deregulation are possible, although the oligopolies of the domestic Japanese industry are likely to remain.

As home and foreign markets are deregulated, financial institutions will have to guard against foreign competitors invading their relatively protected market positions. At the same time they will have to prepare their own strategies to enter foreign markets. Management, marketing and technological prowess will be essential to making these entry strategies successful.

Implementation of advanced technologies

Over $25 billion was spent around the world by financial service organisations on buying in information technology and services in 1988. Double this amount was spent on running and developing their in-house systems. In the mid-1990s this expenditure will exceed $100 billion per year. At about the same time expenditure on computers and telecommunications products and services will exceed 2.2 per cent of world gross product. This figure will be even higher in the developed world, averaging 3–4 per cent of GDP.

Information technology has made possible the emergence of global financial services organisations, which rely totally on communication. That is why global banks are at the forefront of innovation in global communications. The past chairman of Citicorp, the visionary Walter Wriston, summed it up in this way: 'Banking is information.' Financial service organisations use information technology as a competitive weapon to fight their market-share wars with competitors.

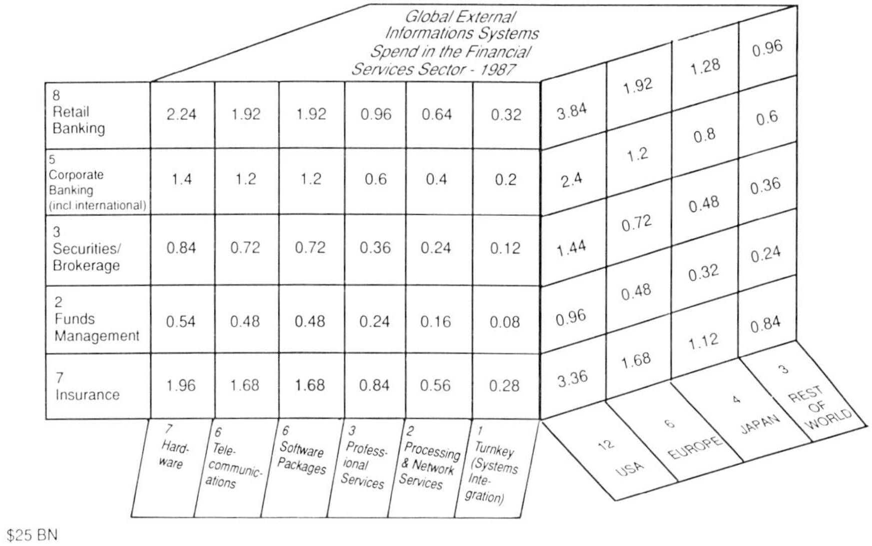

	7 Hard-ware	6 Tele-communic-ations	6 Software Packages	3 Profess-ional Services	2 Processing & Network Services	1 Turnkey (Systems Inte-gration)				
8 Retail Banking	2.24	1.92	1.92	0.96	0.64	0.32	3.84	1.92	1.28	0.96
5 Corporate Banking (incl international)	1.4	1.2	1.2	0.6	0.4	0.2	2.4	1.2	0.8	0.6
3 Securities/ Brokerage	0.84	0.72	0.72	0.36	0.24	0.12	1.44	0.72	0.48	0.36
2 Funds Management	0.54	0.48	0.48	0.24	0.16	0.08	0.96	0.48	0.32	0.24
7 Insurance	1.96	1.68	1.68	0.84	0.56	0.28	3.36	1.68	1.12	0.84

Global External Informations Systems Spend in the Financial Services Sector - 1987

12 USA — 6 EUROPE — 4 JAPAN — 3 REST OF WORLD

$25 BN

Figure 7.2 Global expenditure on bought-in information technology and services by financial institutions in 1987

Yet, surprisingly financial services organisations dissipate a great deal of their capital investment in information technology on failed projects. A 1987 survey of major users of information systems in financial services organisations found that four out of five projects were regarded as failures or failed to live up to expectation.

How do financial service organisations plan for the selection and implementation of new technologies in their businesses? Badly, for the most part, according to several recent studies conducted in North America, Australia and Europe. These studies have shown that the reason so many information–technology-related projects were failures lay in poor planning. The problems arose either because companies did not anticipate users' needs correctly or through a lack of understanding between those planning and running the business and those planning and running the technology. As the following diagram (Figure 7.3) illustrates, successful information systems planning is a complex process and requires several levels of commitment and understanding in an organisation. But top management in financial services will have little option but to tackle this immense waste of vital resources.

Technology will drive the industry to sell and deliver its products through different, technology-based channels such as telemarketing and robotised teller facilities. Integrated relational client databases (where patterns of customer values and choices stimulate real buying decisions for market segments), will be a key to success. At the same time, securitisation (the use of marketable paper instruments to raise finance instead of bank loans) and screen-based,

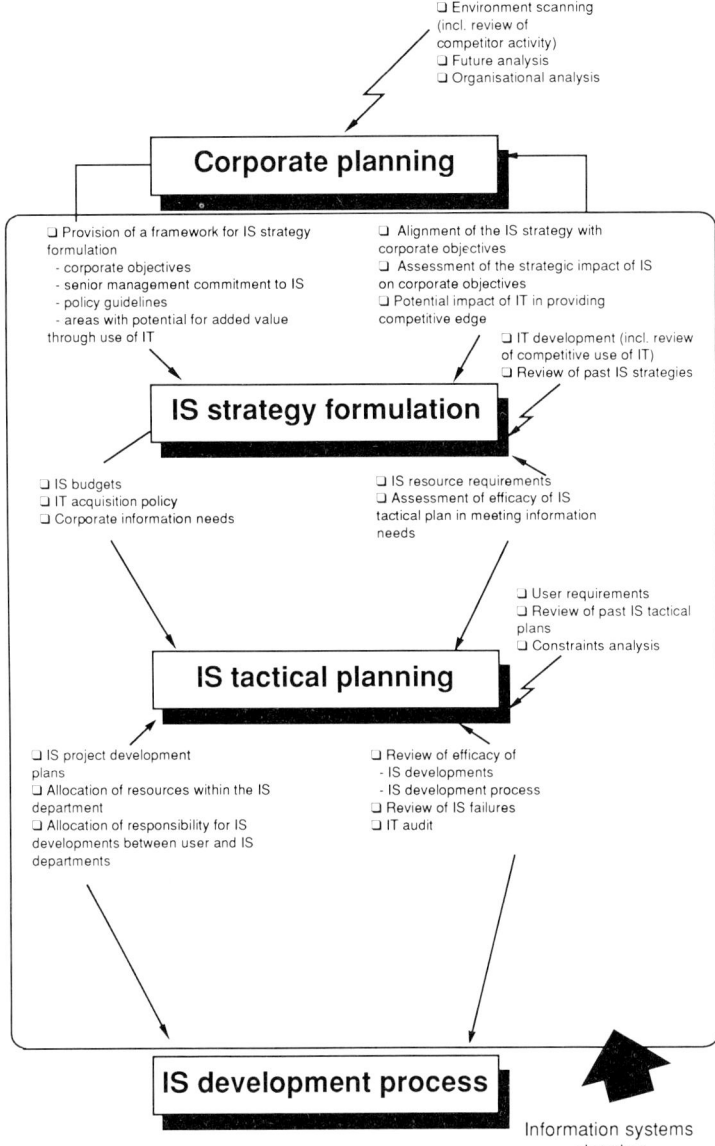

❑ Environment scanning
(incl. review of
competitor activity)
❑ Future analysis
❑ Organisational analysis

Corporate planning

❑ Provision of a framework for IS strategy
formulation
  - corporate objectives
  - senior management commitment to IS
  - policy guidelines
  - areas with potential for added value
through use of IT

❑ Alignment of the IS strategy with
corporate objectives
❑ Assessment of the strategic impact of IS
on corporate objectives
❑ Potential impact of IT in providing
competitive edge
❑ IT development (incl. review
of competitive use of IT)
❑ Review of past IS strategies

IS strategy formulation

❑ IS budgets
❑ IT acquisition policy
❑ Corporate information needs

❑ IS resource requirements
❑ Assessment of efficacy of IS
tactical plan in meeting information
needs

❑ User requirements
❑ Review of past IS tactical
plans
❑ Constraints analysis

IS tactical planning

❑ IS project development
plans
❑ Allocation of resources within the IS
department
❑ Allocation of responsibility for IS
developments between user and IS
departments

❑ Review of efficacy of
  - IS developments
  - IS development process
❑ Review of IS failures
❑ IT audit

IS development process

Information systems
planning

Figure 7.3   The information systems planning process

twenty-four hour global trading have made computerised risk management
essential to major global and regional competitors.

The future of financial service organisations will depend on whether they
have assimilated these trends and are adapting to them. Those to watch are
leading-edge companies such as Citicorp, Chase Manhattan, Banc One,
Wachovia, First National Bank of Chicago, the Bank of Scotland, Crédit

Commercial Français, Union Bank of Finland and Bankorp, all organisations which introduce new technology to drive the rapid generation of new products. The $200 million Fuji Bank electronic banking project also demonstrates the commitment of Japanese banks to catch up with their more automated competitors.

Changing organisational cultures

Another essential for the 1990s is good management of people. Winners must excel in selecting, motivating and retaining business builders. The creation and management of entrepreneurial organisational structures and cultures is particularly important for investment banking and for the sales function in retail and corporate banking.

Although life insurance has been a sales-dominated industry for years, other parts of the financial services world are only just beginning to encourage autonomous profit-centres and individuals.

These companies are now shedding bureaucratic structures. Excess middle management is being removed through early retirement, in large, branch-dominated retail banks. While it is relatively easy to justify paying high compensation to a trader or investment banker who can make the organisation £1 million in profit per year, it is increasingly difficult to justify the top-heavy organisation structures traditional in so many large banks.

Demographic changes in the First World

The pool of young, educated workers needed by traditional financial services is shrinking. It is just as well that financial services organisations will be able to replace this shrinking pool with information technology and systems.

At the same time the emergence of a newly wealthy class is creating a new market for financial services of all kinds, particularly in borrowing for housing, home-related purchases, cars and holidays. Consumers are more demanding than in previous generations and financial services organisations are having to keep up with their demands. This will require more flexible systems for developing and delivering new products. Information technology, particularly database marketing, will be needed to cope with the needs of the new financial consumer.

The shifting balance of power

The debt crisis, which started with the 1983 Polish loan default and grew to alarming proportions during the mid-1980s, reflected the changing economic relations between the First, Second and Third Worlds.

Industrialisation of the Second and Third Worlds, financed by First World capital (some of which involved recycling the Arab petrodollar surplus) has contributed much to the global demand for financial services. It obliged multi-national corporations to take their banks with them to foreign countries and it spread the demand for financial services to countries which hitherto had been completely unbanked.

The era of 'glasnost' and 'perestroika' in Eastern Europe and the USSR and the prospect of liberalisation in the People's Republic of China is gradually opening up the world's two potentially largest marketplaces to foreign competition. In both cases, this may include financial services.

The integration of Western Europe in 1992 may shift the centre of the world stage back to Europe. Although the fast-growing Pacific Rim economies will become increasingly important. The 1990s will see the world's financial services institutions finding great value in taking part in the world's single largest market.

THE FUTURE OF THE FINANCIAL SERVICES INDUSTRY

These six trends will radically alter the face of the financial services industry in a number of ways. First, as a result of changing costs, the industry will split into two types of firm: large, low-cost producers basing their operations on the latest technology, and 'boutiques' with niches in a particular segment of a market.

Industry costs are affected by two trends: human resource costs, including the cost of housing, are rising, while technology costs are falling sharply. The industry will split clearly into global and regional players, because few firms are large enough to benefit from global economies of scale. New technology will accelerate the convergence of different types of financial service operations and produce integrated suppliers of banking, insurance and funds management products.

While financial service organisations get to grips with the relatively new concept of finding out what customers want and using technology to deliver it at a profit, other industries dealing in information are also changing fast. Information providers such as Reuters, Quotron, Telerate, Dunn & Bradstreet, and McGraw-Hill will soon be able to provide not only the information technology itself but also some of the decision support software used in dealing rooms and around the financial institutions.

Global network providers such as GEISCO, AT&T, regional network providers such as NYNEX, and the PTTs are all after the lucrative market for providing financial information and carrying financial transactions.

Sears, Ford, General Motors, Volvo, Mitsubishi and other multi-nationals

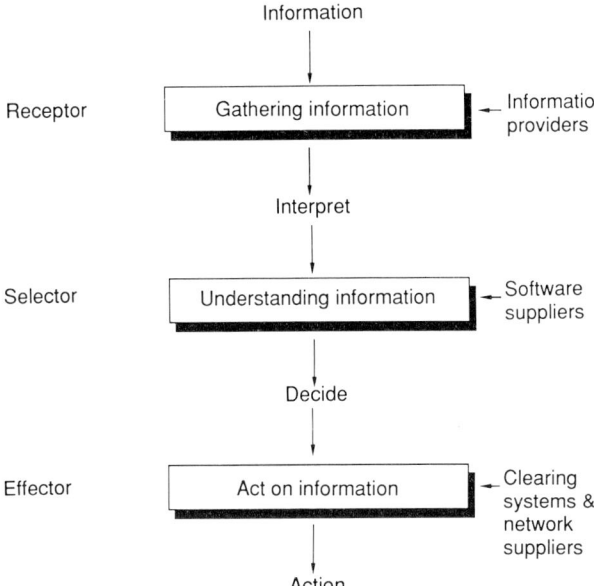

Figure 7.4   The financial services industry as an information management process

rival the traditional financial institutions in financial assets and outlets. Retailers who are particularly interested in electronic funds transfer at point of sale (EFTPOS) have in many countries stolen a march on the banks who proved slower and more conservative.

The financial services industry can be thought of as a three-stage process: the gathering, understanding of and acting upon information, as illustrated by the diagram shown as Figure 7.4..

Some suppliers provide the information-gathering function, others the software or human resource to interpret it, and yet others the delivery systems for acting on it. How far suppliers have penetrated each of these markets varies greatly.

Suppliers have to understand to what extent financial institutions are capable of substituting their services for in-house activities. The trend of financial institutions to contract out a lot of their information management may offer them big opportunities.

So who will win this battle? It is not hard to guess, because sheer size and global representation have already sorted out the winners from the losers. Only around 20 banks are actually big enough to be able to claim that they have a truly global banking mission. The insurance industry will also consolidate so that 20 to 30 players are left on the global field in ten years' time. Some of the contenders are clear already.

At a local level, the winners will be those who have mastered new distribution technologies and created entrepreneurial cultures. Having a large bricks and mortar branch network will be a liability. Low-cost sales and distribution channels will emerge, such as telemarketing, EFTPOS, auto-mated teller machines, visual information systems and home banking. Sophisticated corporate treasury management systems, corporate relationship management and dealing room technology will be essential in the 1990s.

Whatever the type of financial services organisation, it will have to do three things superbly well to succeed:

- understand clients' needs and develop and deliver new products rapidly;
- operate a cost-effective sales and distribution system;
- and manage risk worldwide.

Integrated relational database systems will form the heart of the financial institution. Client information systems, management information systems and risk management systems will be run on such databases. New telecommunications technology will be crucial to the development of financial information. Wide-band, reliable and secure communications channels are needed to handle the enormous volume of traffic, which will flow around financial institutions in the 1990s. All this implies that a lot of work still needs to be done to develop the systems on which financial institutions will depend for their daily bread in 2000.

8

MARKETING ON THE MOVE

'Cheaper computer power has helped fuel the remarkable growth of direct marketing in recent years. Companies in all industry sectors are taking advantage of the opportunities to target small customer segments accurately. But developing an efficient marketing database requires changes in attitudes and approaches', says Alan Bigg, Chairman, Christian Brann.

The marketing man, marketing and marketing methods are moving targets. By their very nature, marketing people are always seeking new ideas. What brand manager ever got famous by keeping the same advertising?

As a very new discipline compared with long established practices like finance or production, marketing has not had time to become codified or traditionalised. Nor have the techniques and processes of marketing, many of which seem to be in constant flux. In the media of marketing, for example, television advertising has replaced press as the major medium for food advertisers. Colour magazines with newspapers have formed a whole new advertising category. The magazine market is unrecognisable from the time when four giant weeklies dominated the media planning scene. Satellite and cable TV are now poised for take-off.

Promotion techniques have changed too. At one stage every detergent pack had a plastic daffodil. (Whatever happened to plastic-daffodil manufacturers?) At one time point-of-sale merchandising was big business; now it is circumscribed by the power of the big retailers. Public relations has waxed and waned and waxed again in the marketing armoury. New dimensions to the marketing mix are constantly coming to the fore. Design, for example, is a current hot topic. Yet the hottest of all current subjects, and the one which will cause the biggest changes in marketing departments since the invention of qualitative research, is the rise and rise of direct marketing; a rise that is not just a matter of historical fact but also of unanimous prediction.

This rise will have many effects. Perhaps the most important is that at last the marketer will be able to deliver the promise that his activities will be customer-driven. While some activities will be planned on a national or regional basis in support of product actions, the heart of the marketing plan will be a myriad of individually tailored communication programmes, triggered by the customer's own actions, programmes that will only exist inside the marketing department's own computer.

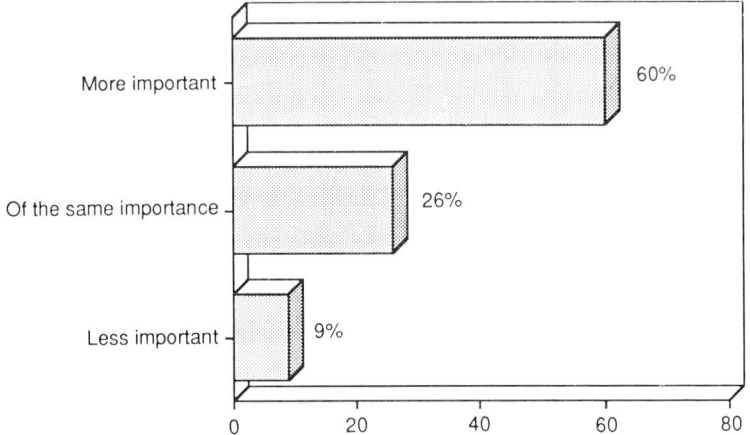

Figure 8.1 Response of major UK advertisers to the question: 'Will direct marketing be more important/less important than image advertising to your company by the year 2000?' (*Source* Christian Brann Limited/Campaign Survey 1988)

That is a pretty ambitious claim for something that is still seen by many as the poor relation of 'proper' marketing. But the stampede by the major advertising chains to get into direct marketing underlines the threat that exists to conventional thinking. Yet only recently direct marketing was a rather esoteric speciality, full of strange gurus and mysterious rules. It was the exclusive province of the mail order people and to most mainstream advertisers it was 'that *Reader's Digest* stuff.'

GROWTH DRIVEN BY COMPUTER

So why is direct marketing now the fastest-growing branch of marketing both in the US and in Europe? Why have the mainstream agencies been rushing to set up direct marketing subsidiaries? Why have so many major advertisers switched large chunks of their promotional spends into direct marketing? The answer lies, as it does so often today, in the computer.

At the heart of today's direct marketing campaigns will be a list of customers or of prospects. The more information there is on that list the more effective the direct marketing will be, because it can be used to target the right offer to the right customer at the right time. And today's computers can increasingly analyse and use that information more cost-effectively.

The cost of storing and processing data has fallen by a factor of 400 in 20 years. Compare that as a key cost component of direct marketing with the astonishing escalation in the cost of producing TV commercials (150 per cent in five years in the UK).

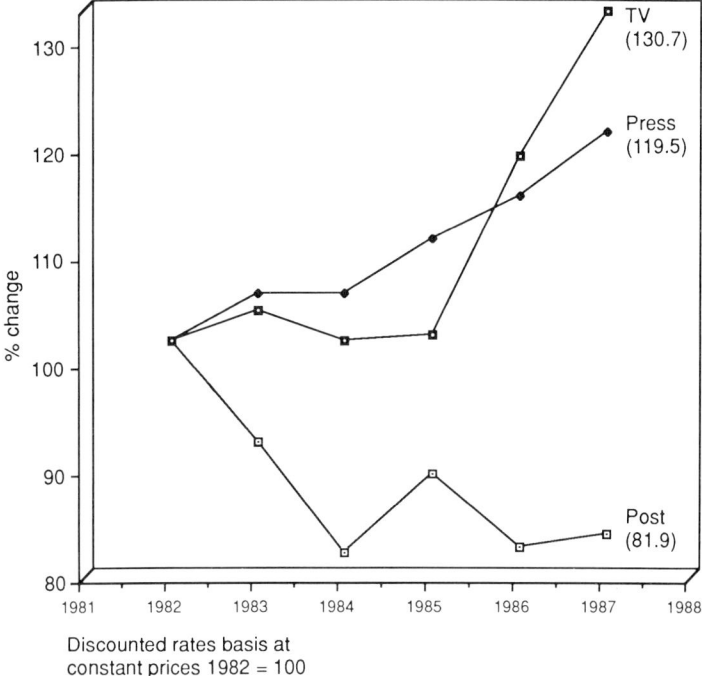

Figure 8.2 Cost reductions and relative cost inflation. Index of media cost infltation 1982–1987 (*Source: Advertising Statistics Yearbook 1988*)

Couple that with the fact that postage costs have risen at a far slower rate than media space costs and it is no wonder that more and more advertisers are finding that it is cost-effective to communicate directly and personally with their target market.

Another factor in today's marketing that has accelerated the growth in direct marketing is the trend towards segmentation. Few markets are mass markets any more. More and more companies are segmenting their product lines so as to ensure that they have really strong appeals to particular groups of customers. While the mass media have fragmented to an extent, they do not offer a cost effective way of reaching small, highly individual target markets. As a consequence many advertisers are taking advantage of direct marketing's ability to deliver different messages to different audiences.

But the cost factors and the changes in product lines are relatively insignificant compared to the power that has been put into the marketing departments' hands by the arrival of the marketing database. The advances in affordable techniques to hold and analyse data have brought a new dimension to the whole process of building customer sales–a dimension that few companies are even beginning to exploit.

To see what this potential is, it is necessary first of all to distinguish between two things: the marketing database and database marketing. The *marketing database* is a computer-held file of all the information available about the behaviour of existing and potential customers. This will include not just demographic data, such as age and household composition, but also information about past purchasing behaviour and reactions to previous promotions. *Database marketing* takes this information goldmine and uses it to optimise marketing communications. As yet few companies have really exploited the power that a marketing database brings. But as more companies begin to realise the opportunities, the pace of change is accelerating. In some market sectors the marketing database becomes very effective very rapidly. British banks for instance, are investing heavily in marketing databases as a means of warding off the challenge of the building societies and insurance conglomerates.

CHANGING ATTITUDES

The introduction of a database clearly offers great opportunities but the process is not a simple one. For a start it involves the setting aside of a lot of traditional practices. Moreover, the decision to set up a database is an unusual one for a marketing person, because the timelag between the substantial investment and pay off is longer than with conventional marketing investments. Few companies have come to regret the decision, however. Once the database is established, it enables them to transform parts of their marketing effort.

Among the principal benefits are that they can:

- work relatively unobserved by their competitors;
- introduce new and specialised products without the vast costs of consumer launches and sales force training;
- control the timing of their promotion very precisely;
- control who gets which message – it is no longer necessary to subsidise existing customers by offering them promotions aimed at attracting new customers.

Direct marketing the database way produces a significant change in the way that marketing is carried on. Marketing has always been based on probabilities. For example, 'It is probable that an AB under 35 will want to buy this product', or 'It is more probable that people who live in the South will be able to find the product in the shops'. Once the database is developed, probability gives away to certainty. 'This offer is going to people who have bought children's clothing in the last six months'. 'This product has particular advantages over competitor A's product: we'll aim it at those who have that product at home'.

Another important certainty that comes from the direct marketing approach is the ability to tell which parts of the activity are contributing effectively. You can measure the results both immediately (how many responses? how many sales?) and in in the longer term (what is the lifetime value of this customer?) While it is not always possible to explain why things have or have not worked, the simple knowledge of what has happened enables the marketing team to build future plans with much greater confidence. The activity is, in a sense, self-researching.

This added certainty means that most companies which have decided to adopt the direct or database approach are steadily increasing the percentage of their promotional budgets that they devote to it.

BUILDING THE DATABASE

Developing and using a marketing database is a four stage process, as Figure 8.3 shows.

While a substantial investment will be required to set up a database and so make direct marketing effective, the decision is not one that has to be taken as an act of faith.

Typically, organisations both large and small start with a study to identify the potential. They will carry out some test mailings and advertising in order to see whether the approach begins to work for them and then commit themselves to develop the technique over a two- to three-year period.

The most crucial decision is how the marketing database should be constructed and how it can interrelate with all the other information that an organisation collects. This problem is particularly difficult for those companies which moved into computing at an early stage. Virtually every bank and insurance company worldwide is attempting to restructure its computer systems to meet the new demands of the marketing department. The restraining factors are not just technology or investment cost. Possibly the most serious restraint, is the serious shortage of experienced people to handle the work that is generated.

In many companies the use of the technique is being driven by bright middle managers who do not have direct marketing experience but who see the

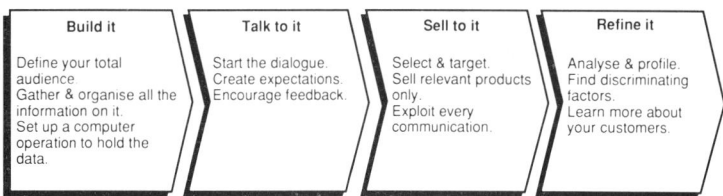

Figure 8.3   The four stages of developing a database

(a)

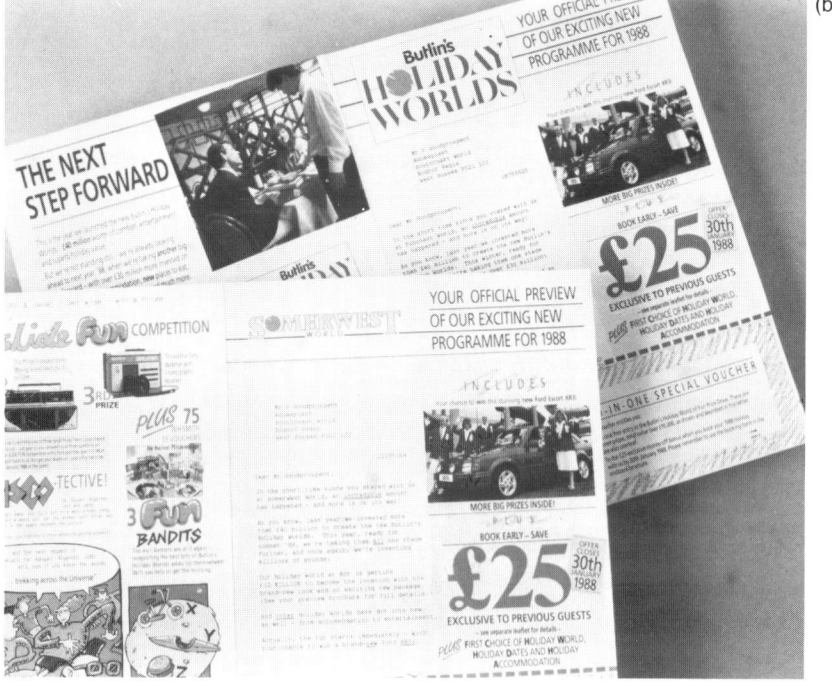

(b)

(c)

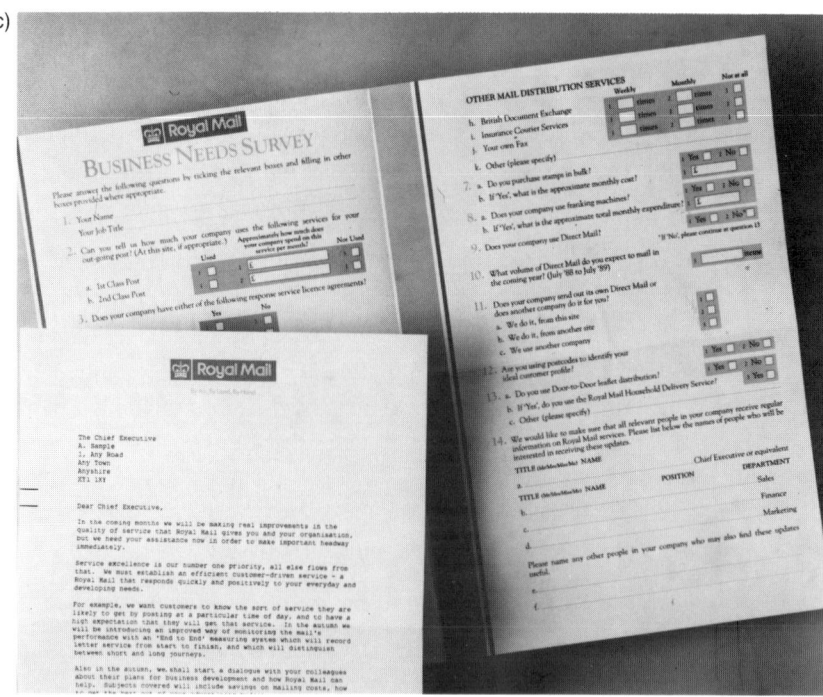

(d)

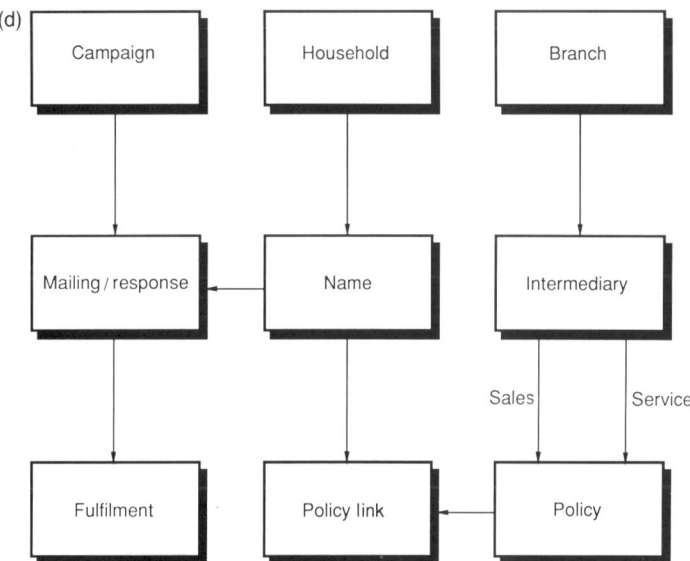

Figure 8.4 Future marketing winners
(a) Barclays Bank targets tone of voice for affluent marrieds and teenagers.
(b) Butlin's use electronic printing to send appropriate messages to previous guests.
Children's names are used, and reference is made to previous holidays.
(c) The Royal Mail gathers data for improving its service to business customers.
(d) Logical data model.

opportunities and make it their personal mission to bring it into their company. This is in many ways more effective than importing an outsider because the switch in habits that is demanded by direct marketing requires considerable knowledge of how a company works. It impacts heavily on sales and computer departments and on many administrative and accounting functions, too.

THE SERVICE MARKET – BUYER BEWARE!

Not surprisingly, the boom in the use of direct marketing has brought a corresponding boom among the service providers. The services required are more diverse than in others forms of marketing and their management is more complex. They require both strategic and creative thinking together with specialist computing expertise.

The area is something of a minefield and great care is necessary to choose the right partners, both in terms of size and capability. Because the issues are so complex, companies should take care to investigate the depth of expertise offered by some service providers.

The current growth of direct marketing is based largely upon the success it is achieving. There seems little doubt that it will continue to take a larger share of the marketing budget as new electronic media arrive and as techniques and expertise improve and as technology marches on.

Almost every company, regardless of its exisiting distribution channels, needs to look seriously at introducing direct marketing to its business. Once your competitors have set up a database and are communicating regularly with customers on a personal basis and with relevantly targetted products you will be at a serious disadvantage if you cannot do so.

The marketing winners of the 1990s will be those who most effectively harness this new medium (see Figure 8.4).

9

BUSINESS USES OF ECONOMIC FORECASTING

'Forecasting is both one of the most useful and most mistrusted of business activities. Advances in computing will bring forecasting techniques to more and more managers' desks in the coming decades. But, unless the manager who uses these techniques understands their limitations and how they work, he risks making costly errors', says Frank Gelber, Director of Economic and Building Services, BIS Shrapnel.

In the extraordinarily volatile economic environment of the last 20 years, it is increasingly crucial for businesses to understand the implications of developments in the economy. The pace of change in the environment facing individual businesses is accelerating. Strategic issues which could once be viewed in terms of a fixed environment now require an understanding of developments in the environment itself. Growth cycles in different parts of the economy, either internally driven or generated by economic policy, affect most industries.

Economic forecasting's usefulness to business lies in helping managers plan effectively, to avoid major errors caused by the expectation that the future will continue like the immediate past. It also aids them in identifying opportunities for expansion or investment (or divestment) when the market has overreacted.

Businesses now use economic forecasting widely and routinely to support planning and decision-making. But forecasters cannot tell the future with certainty. Inevitably, forecasts are subject to a margin of error which can vary according to circumstances. Given the inherent unpredictability of the future it is not surprising that many managers ask themselves questions such as: How useful are such forecasts? What are the merits of the alternative forecasting techniques? What are the likely developments in future methods of economic forecasting?

This chapter attempts to answer those questions, starting with how useful forecasts can be.

HOW USEFUL ARE FORECASTS?

From the many attempts to evaluate the performance of economic and business forecasting, several lessons have emerged:

- Some assumptions or forecasts about the future are necessary for business planning and decision-making.
- Some aspects of the future can be predicted more accurately than others.
- Some techniques are better than others.
- Uncertainty remains a fact of life. Forecasting errors are inevitable.

These lessons emphasise the need for realistic expectations of what economic forecasting can contribute to business. More sophisticated users have learned to assess risk by analysing the implications of alternative scenarios.

WHAT FORECASTING METHODS ARE AVAILABLE?

There are three broad methodological approaches to economic forecasting for business.

Econometric forecasting models

A decade ago there was considerable enthusiasm and optimism for the application of econometric modelling techniques to forecasting. While these techniques are now in common use and, in appropriate circumstances, provide powerful forecasting tools, actual achievements have fallen short of earlier expectations. Econometric forecasting models essentially project past patterns of behaviour and relationships into the future in a statistically unbiased way. Problems arise if changes occur over time in the structure or relationships the company is interested in or if new influences become important. Changes in economic and social structures have been particularly important during the 1980s. Because the pace of change is unlikely to slow, this will affect the length of time for which econometric forecasting models remain valid.

Judgemental forecasting

Judgemental forecasting methods remain popular and can be quite powerful when performed by experts in the relevant field. There are, however, dangers in judgemental forecasting:

- Forecasting by committee tends to produce middle-of-the-range comprom-ise forecasts rather than most likely outcomes.
- Judgemental forecasts can also be subject to bias, for example, arising from wishful thinking.

On the one hand, judgemental forecasting methods tend to be more expensive than quantitative techniques, because they cannot be automated and therefore require greater expert input. On the other, the benefits of good forecasting input make this expense minor. Accordingly, it is essential to identify forecasters with good judgement.

Non-extrapolative methods

This category encompasses a wide and growing range of techniques of varying scientific standing, such as visionary forecasts, scenario analysis and environ-mental scanning. While futurism may offer little clear benefit to business, there may be times, particularly for long-range forecasting applications, when a more creative or imaginative approach is needed to supplement or contrast with traditional extrapolative methods.

Research into the relative performance of different techniques in all three categories has revealed that:

- no forecasting method consistently outperforms all others;
- highly sophisticated techniques are not necessarily superior to simpler techniques;
- forecasts tend to be more useful when they are transparent, that is, when the underlying logic or rationale is clear. A rule of thumb is to believe only those forecasts for which you know the causal mechanism and can accept it as reasonable. Blind faith in sophisticated techniques can be fatal.

HOW FORECASTS CAN BE USED

Economic forecasts are most commoly used in business to support planning and decision-making. The main applications are as follows.

1 Strategic planning (longer-term forecasting)

This refers particularly to investment decisions, whether by acquisition or expansion of capacity. In the case of investment in new plant and equipment it is crucial to know the size of the market when the equipment is ready for use and the level of demand likely to prevail over the operating life of equipment. Managers making these investment decisions must understand the cyclical nature of the market, its volatility and whether current levels of activity are likely to increase or decrease in the long-term sense.

Specific applications include:

- Acqusition strategies and the timing of acquisitions.
- Expansion/investment in new capacity, including timing and assumptions for assessing feasibility. This is particularly important in the light of long lead times in many investment projects and the need to understand market conditions when the investment is completed. Examples include commercial buildings and expansion or installation of capacity in industries where viability is influenced by demand, exchange rates, interest rates, inflation or competitiveness.
- Cyclical influences on financing decisions. Interest rates fluctuate over time depending on conditions in the overall economy. In this respect it is necessary to assess longer-term influences on interest rates. The influences include both the inflationary environment and short-term political influences, such as the use of monetary policy to achieve economic objectives.

2   Budgeting/planning (short-run forecasting)

Economic influences on product demand and economic conditions provide an essential input in:

- the use of demand forecasting models in market growth, and demand forecasting and inflation of costs as an input to marketing strategy and pricing. Market growth and demand elasticities are important here.
- production, inventory and labour force planning.
- setting budgets and priorities.
- financial forecasting, including interest rate and exchange rate management (timing and exposure).

3   Investment decisions

Many areas of investment are dominated by financial flows and are highly cyclical. In these cases, economic forecasting can help to identify expected returns, risk margins, prices and prospects. The objective is to understand when markets are out of equilibrium. The essential ingredient is an understanding of the fundamentals as opposed to current market conditions and an identification of turning points in the cycle.

For example, the long lead-times in construction of large buildings combine with flows of investment funds to produce strong cycles in building and property markets. It is not uncommon for building at the peak of the cycle to be between two and four times the level of building in the trough, with a corresponding cycle in prices and rents. When planning to construct or invest in a building project, it is essential to predict the likely demand for space and the likely rents and yields when the project is completed between two and four years hence. These conditions can be markedly different from now. At the same time, there are counter-cyclical opportunities at the bottom of the market. There are also opportunities when the market is strong. But it can be disastrous to be caught in a market downturn. Counter-cyclical investment strategies can be highly profitable.

Economic inputs of these kinds can be used, not only by professional investment houses and companies, but also by individuals as a means of building personal wealth and superannuation.

Other uses of economic forecasting include:

- quantitative assessment of economic impacts or needs for use as the basis of cases in advocacy, both as evidence in court and for use in lobbying governments;
- provision of economic arguments and material for use in publicity and marketing etc.

MATCHING FORECASTING METHODS WITH APPLICATIONS

The appropriate forecasting technique will depend on both the application and the nature of the market under consideration. In this section we highlight the choices with three examples.

1   *Coping with the business cycle*

Industrial nations have always experienced cyclical fluctuations in the level of economic activity. Expansion occurs at around the same time in a number of economic variables. Eventually this gives way to a general decline. However, the timing and pattern of the cyclical fluctuations are not necessarily regular.

- Econometric forecasting models have not been overly successful in predicting turning points in economic actvity.
- Judgemental forecasts can perform better in this area, particularly when supplemented by an analysis of the particular circumstances.
- Certain economic variables tend to lead the general business cycle. While there is no single ideal leading indicator, relevant ones include stock levels, share prices, interest rates, credit growth and telephone connections. An

index of relevant leading indicators can provide a valuable adjunct to judgemental forecasts of cyclical fluctuations in economic activity.

In addition to the business cycle, it has been claimed that longer-run cycles in economic activity exist. For example, according to the Kondratieff Long Wave Theory, western economies are subject to cycles of 40 to 60 years in duration. Recently there has been renewed interest in such long-run cyclical theories. However, the existence of such cycles remains unproven. Economies are subject to longer-run expansions and contractions, but there is no uniformity in the timing of such movements. We remain sceptical of 'black box' theories unless there is a good explanation of why they should work.

Using our example of building activity and property markets again, cyclical fluctuations in building activity, rents and values are integrally associated with

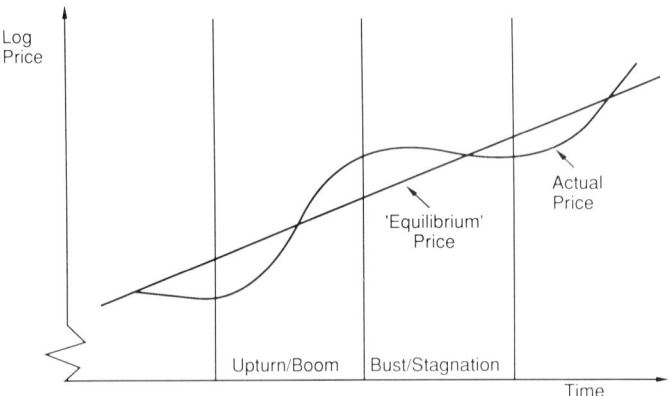

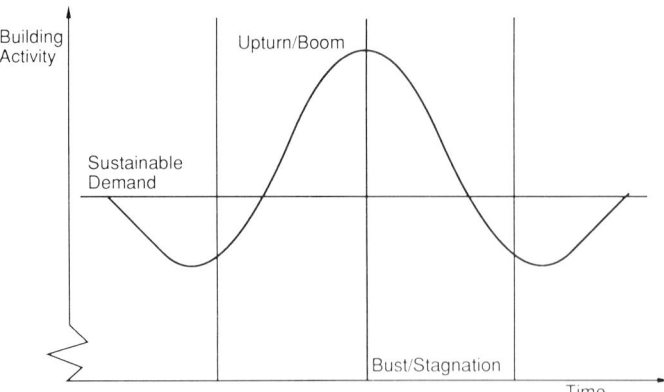

Figure 9.1   Price and activity in the building investment cycle – illustrative charts

financial capital flows into and out of investment in property. The long-term 'warranted' or 'sustainable' level of building activity depends on the 'underlying' demand, which is determined by longer-run economic and demographic factors. But actual levels fluctuate around these levels, with a corresponding cycle in values. Meanwhile, the building cycle can continue under its own momentum out of kilter with the fundamentals for long periods. The key to the market is to understand the fundamentals of underlying demand. For example, the underlying demand for housing depends on household formation and demographics, while the underlying demand for office space depends on office employment and space per employee.

The extent of deficiency or surplus of stock will determine the magnitude of the upturn or downturn. The timing of the turning point is often triggered by economic factors such as movement in interest rates or cycles in economic activity which affect short-term demand for space. In this case, forecasts of building and property markets use economic techniques to assess underlying demand and the magnitude of the cyclical move, but use judgemental techniques based on forecasts of economic conditions to predict the timing of the turning point. The accompanying diagrams illustrate the cyclical nature of property markets (Figure 9.1, 9.2, 9.3).

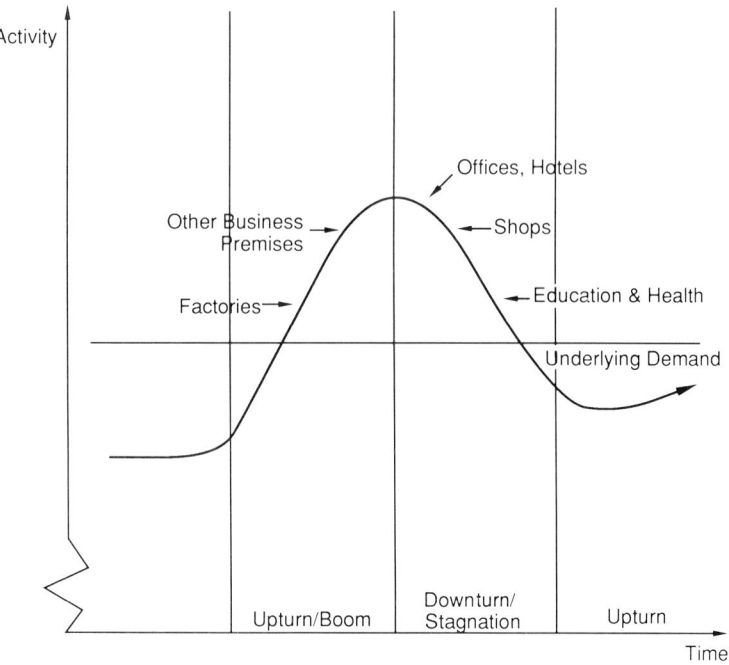

Figure 9.2   Non-dwelling building in Australia–stage of cycle at September 1988

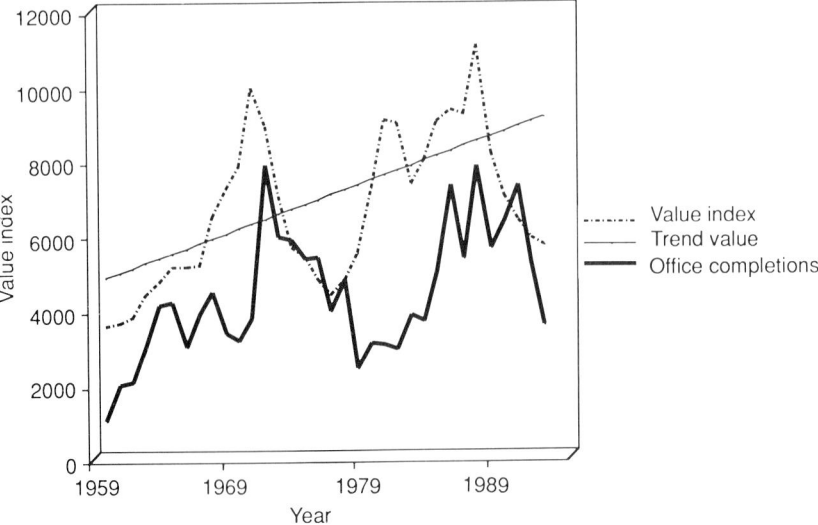

Figure 9.3   The New South Wales commercial property cycle in constant 1987 dollars

2   *Forecasting exchange rates*

Following the widespread adoption of floating exchange rates, intense efforts have been devoted to forecasting short-term currency movements. Although businesses clearly need forecasts of future exchange rates this is an area where economic forecasting has generally had little success. Actual exchange rate movements have been substantial and often unpredicted during the 1980s (see Figure 9.4).

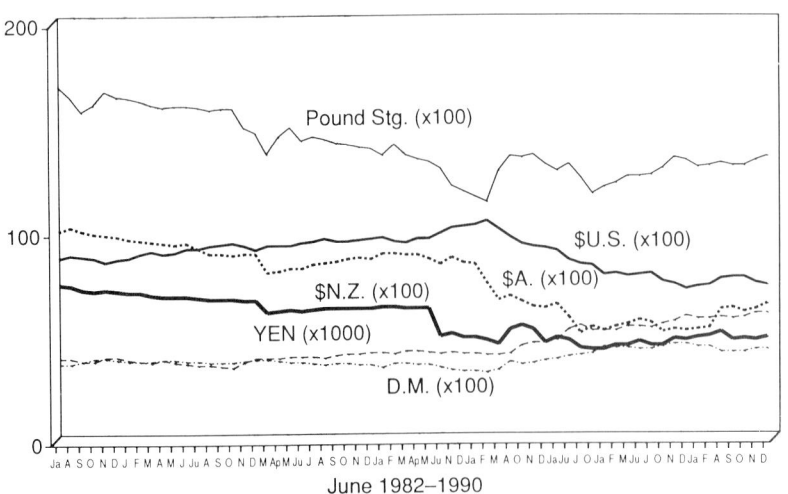

Figure 9.4   Fluctuation of exchange rates (*Source:* BIS Shrapnel Pty, Limited)

Part of the problem is that there is no settled economic theory to explain how exchange rates are determined. According to received doctrine, exchange rates move over the longer run to bring into balance the prices of internationally traded goods in different countries. However, the foreign exchange markets have become notorious for 'overshooting'. Also, while, in the longer term, exchange rates tend to conform to 'purchasing power parity' forecasts, empirical studies have revealed that short-term fluctuations in exchange rates follow a 'random walk'. This may mean that exchange rates have an equal probability of rising or falling in the short run. There will be a continuing demand for, and supply of, exchange rate forecasts. However, at the same time, forecasters and decision-makers will have to come to grips with the margins of error involved. The role of the economist here may be to remind participants of the risks involved and the specialised nature of the market.

3 *Forecasting product demand*

Business planning revolves around expected future sales. This is an area in which economic forecasters have been particularly helpful. There is a variety of alternative forecasting techniques from which to choose, but not all techniques are equally successful in different circumstances.

Relatively simple econometric models can provide a valuable forecasting tool in some circumstances. For example, most of the year-to-year fluctuation in sales of stoves in Australia can be explained by a model which relates the demand for stoves to the following explanatory variables:

- the number of dwellings constructed
- real expenditure on other consumer durables (excluding appliances) as a reference cycle
- percentage change in employment, *and*
- a time trend.

Figure 9.5 reveals a reasonably good fit between model estimates and actual sales over part years. Forecasts are readily generated by inserting forecasts of the explanatory variables into the model.

A relatively straightforward, but extremely powerful technique is to identify demand for a product by particular groups of end-users. A model of the prospects for each end-user sector then generates demand forecasts. In most cases this is more powerful than econometric techniques, but it cannot be used to estimate price elasticities. For example, concrete can be modelled in relation to its end-uses in residential building, non-residential building (offices, shops, hotels, etc.) and non-building construction (roads, dams, mines, etc.)

The total demand for concrete depends on the overall level of building activity, but forecasting models based on past relationships between aggregate

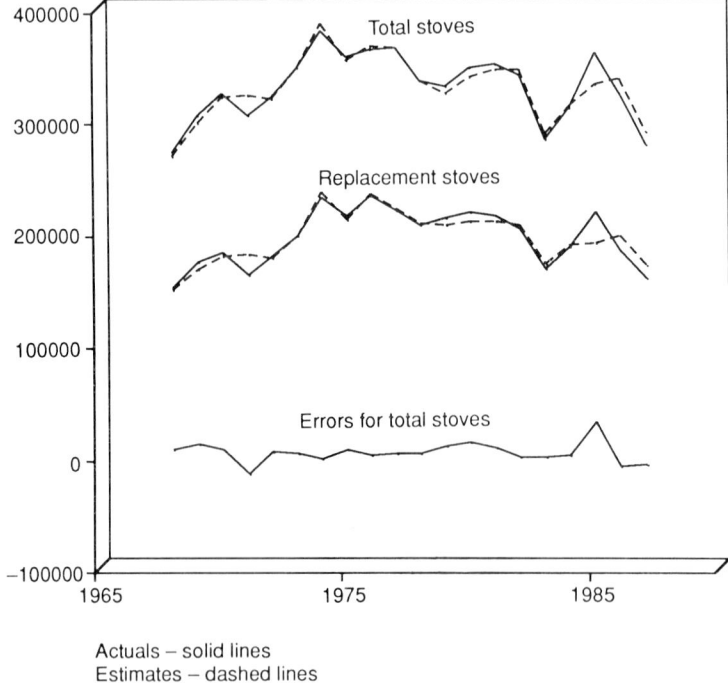

Actuals – solid lines
Estimates – dashed lines

Figure 9.5   Demand for stoves–actual vs. estimated values

building activity and concrete usage can be subject to quite large errors. This arises because concrete usage varies substantially across the different sectors of the building industry and because growth is typically not evenly spread across those sectors. As illustrated in Table 9.1, more accurate forecasts of the total demand for concrete can be prepared by disaggregation into end-use sectors and by estimating how much each sector will need. These forecasts should be checked through time against historical data to ensure that they track well.

One pitfall in forecasting product demand on the basis of historical relationships arises from the varying market penetration of a product during its life cycle. The market penetration of a wide range of products follows an

Table 9.1   Demand for concrete (cubic metres)

Activity level in end-use sectors	Sector usage coefficients	Sector demand
House building (S_1)	U_1	S_1U_1
Other residental building (S_2)	U_2	S_2U_2
Renovation (S_3)	U_3	S_3U_3
Commercial and industrial building (S_4)	U_4	S_4U_4
Social and institutional building (S_5)	U_5	S_5U_5
Other constructions (S_6)	U_6	S_6U_6
Total demand	$\sum_{i=1}^{6}$	S_iU_i

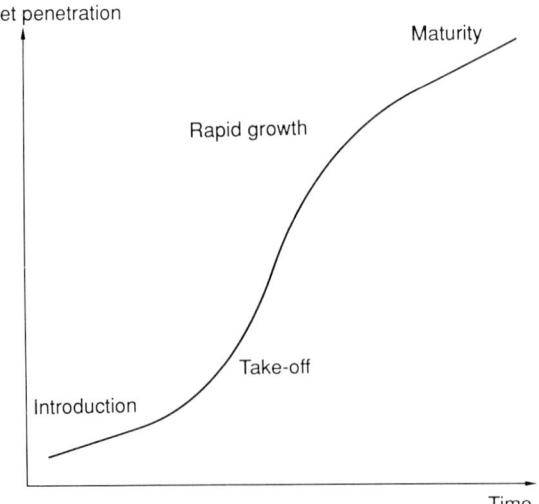

Figure 9.6   Typical product life cycle

S-shaped path over time. This reflects a number of different stages: introduction and recognition, rapid growth and finally maturity (Figure 9.6). The time span of the product life cycle can vary enormously from product to product. For example, while the cycle for some products, such as video cassette recorders, can be measured in years, others, such as consumption of coal as the dominant energy source, need to be measured in decades or even longer periods.

THE FUTURE FOR FORECASTING

Economic forecasting became a growth industry during the 1960s and 1970s as a result of the combination of major changes in the economic environment, increased uncertainty, and advances in statistical techniques arising from the wider availability of computers. However, the scientific status and prestige of forecasting was damaged during the 1970s and 1980s by the pace of change and the emergence of serious forecasting errors. Nonetheless, forecasting, especially for business applications, is expected to continue to grow in importance over the next decade. This reflects a number of factors:

- increasing numbers of managers who are trained and interested in quantitative forecasting techniques;
- wider availability of cheaper and more powerful computers;
- increased data availability, providing both the potential and the means of better forecasting;
- greater emphasis on planning and forecasting in decision-making.

This does not necessarily imply that forecasting accuracy will improve. No matter how sophisticated forecasting techniques become, they will not eliminate uncertainty. More realistic perceptions will emerge of the strengths and weaknesses of forecasting procedures. Both forecasters and decision-makers will learn to accept and cope with uncertainty in the future economic environment.

At the same time, forecasting is becoming increasingly specialised in tune with increases in the amount of research required to keep pace with developments, both in the economy and in specific markets. In many firms, the cost has led companies to close their research functions in favour of using external specialists, who spread costs across users. Research companies can also help in the internal forecasting process. They can provide a variety of services from end-use sector demand to briefing managers on the prospects for the economic environment, as useful inputs to strategic planning.

The use of forecasting activities is now in the ascendency in business, non-profit and public sector organisation. In future, forecasters will gain greater status but they will be more appropriately viewed as helpful advisers rather than prophets.

CONCLUSIONS – AN EXECUTIVE SUMMARY

■ In the rapidly changing economic environment of the 1970s and 1980s, economic forecasting and briefings on economic conditions has become an essential ingredient to the budgeting, planning and strategy formulation process, particularly in markets subject to cyclical fluctuations. These roles will continue to expand in the uncertain and rapidly changing environment of the 1990s, as companies learn to use the information better.

■ Quantitative forecasting techniques took a quantum leap in the 1970s with the advent of cheap computer power and large-scale models. It became possible to undertake estimation techniques that would formerly have been prevented by computation time. Large-scale models were built that allowed researchers to estimate economy-wide impact of specified changes in the environment. Further innovations in this type of estimation techniques are unlikely. The developments of the 1990s will be refinements of existing techniques, with most progress being made on better use of forecasts.

■ Different techniques have different strengths and weaknesses. It is important to choose appropriate techniques to suit the application.

■ Forecasting and briefings on economic conditions are becoming increasingly specialised. There is a danger here. Government policies, general economic conditions and individual sectors of the economy are all closely interrelated. Ignoring these interrelationships is to court disaster. 'Industry analysts' cannot afford to ignore the outside world.

- Companies will continue to cut back on costly internal forecasting units in favour of outside consultants with appropriate expertise. At the same time, company use of forecasting is moving to higher levels of management, as top management recognises the importance of economic and market information in strategy formulation.

- Economic forecasts are inevitably subject to forecasting error and unforeseen events. Managers need to recognise how much confidence they can place in specific forecasts. If something happens which affects the forecasts, the task of the forecaster is to let his client know quickly. This should be part of the brief.

- Forecasting has a relatively small role to play in industries which are relatively stable. However, these industries are becoming scarce. In other sectors, where change is more rapid, it will have a much larger role because the survivors have usually learnt the importance of planning for business cycles.

- The forecaster must understand both the nature of economic conditions as they affect specific markets and the importance of likely changes in conditions. In cyclical markets, the forecaster's job is to have a long memory, to remember the fundamentals and to place current market conditions in a time perspective. Here he has a briefing role as well as a forecasting role.

10

ELECTRONIC IMAGING: THE THIRD WAVE OF INFORMATION PROCESSING

'Computer technology is at a crossroads. It can either pursue the elusive goal of intelligence, or it can focus on electronic imaging. The latter will have the greatest impact', says Raimund Wasner Senior Vice President CAP International, because it is closest to the way people prefer to handle information.

It seems incongruous that after 2000 years and fantastic advances in technology the printed page is still the final image of all our thoughts and efforts. But it is. And in spite of what the majority of Information Age pundits say it will continue to be so because paper is the accepted, effective and convenient way in which humans communicate. Computers and communications networks have brought information to our fingertips but it takes people, pencil and paper to explain it. Putting it on paper is still the most widely accepted form of communication. The near-term challenge is not to make paper go away, rather it is to integrate paper-based information systems with digital ones. The acceptance, effectiveness and convenience of paper is the result of learning, teaching, training and thousands of years of history. The learning process has reinforced the mind's ability to focus first on the whole and then the pieces. The mind absorbs an entire page at a time. For it, a page is a single image of thought, a synthesis, a construction. People can prioritise information on a page.

Computers, on the other hand, at present prioritise nothing. They are dumb, are programmed to operate linearly, to perform rote functions quickly. Even with the blessings of artificial intelligence, in the bizarre world of computers it is entirely possible to have an intelligent babbling idiot on your desktop. The famous, grammatically correct overheard computer utterance. 'Colourless green ideas sleep furiously' exemplifies the simultaneous intelligence and lunacy of the wonderful world of computers. The computer still likes its information a character at a time, albeit in very large numbers and at great speeds. Most importantly, unlike a person, the computer exercises no element of choice in consumption. For it, information is based on processing strings of characters; the synthesised image remains undefined.

Indeed, we measure computer storage and processing capability by the number of characters it can handle. Bits, bytes, megabits, megabytes, gigabytes, all count in thousands and millions the number of disjointed individual characters capable of being stored or displayed by a machine. The only form of organisation for all those characters is provided by a primitive structure of file names. Nothing clearly differentiates documents from programs, sales figures from invoices, poems from doodles. On one hand computers grow in ability to store and process more information more rapidly. On the other hand the increased ability to capture, store, retrieve, analyse and process data actually results in creating more information rather than reducing it.

Experts initially expected computers to make a tremendous impact on the office environment by reducing the dependence on paper. But so far computers have had little impact on the paper trail other than to increase consumption by some 300 billion pages a year.

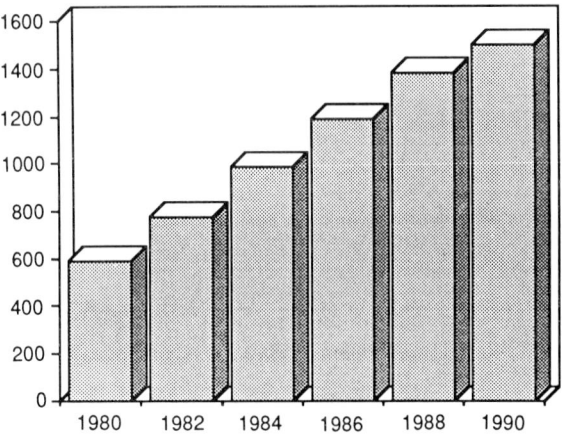

Figure 10.1   Pages printed in US offices (in billions of pages)
Source: *GAP International 1988*

This information processing challenge has created a great need for white collar workers to become proficient at handling information management resources, such as copiers, printers, computers, scanners, mass storage devices and a plethora of software. Half of the US work force is occupied in this kind of work. So much so that half of the 60 million desks in American business have some kind of a keyboard on them. That is a lot of information at a lot of fingertips, not to mention a lot of paper. This 'knowledge worker' must become sophisticated at extracting, distributing, storing and communicating information on paper.

Hundreds of millions of dollars have been spent in vain on bypassing that

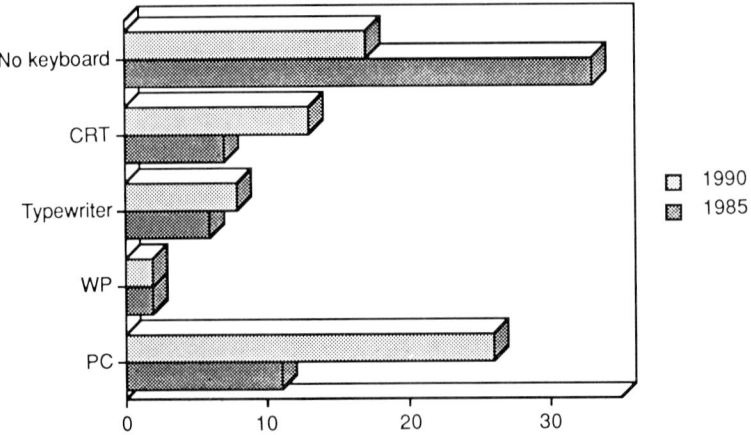

Figure 10.2 Keyboard dependence by white collar workforce

step. The US newspaper industry alone spent around $200 million on videotex ventures designed to break away from distributing the composed page in favour of immediate electronic display. The conclusion from the four years of experiments was that computer technology and electronic distribution is not a current or near-term threat to newspaper publishing. Why? The answer is remarkably simple. A study of how people go about reading a newspaper, scanning the entire edition a page at a time to focus on areas of interest, shows that the process is completely out of step with the way in which computers can economically present information. While computers like information a character at a time, people like several pages at a time.

Every advance in technology brings with it tremendous gains in information processing. What computers do best is put characters on forests of paper. They can generate, reduce, distribute, store, print and regurgitate far more information than we can. Not only can they do it much faster, they can do so much of it that it is impossible to process it by current means. The meaningful information that can be processed must be given the final distinction of being put on paper. The output is produced by computer but is now, ironically, furthest away from computer readability, particularly when colour, graphics, photography and drawings are added. This in part explains why, despite great expense, only 1 per cent of the information needs of a business are in electronic form and 99 per cent remain on paper.

The gap between the way computer stores, represent and communicate information and the way people do the same things, makes up a large part of near-term technology opportunity. The conversion of images to computer-readable form and the conversion of computer images to human-readable form are at the fulcrum of the office equipment market.

A CROSSROADS FOR COMPUTER TECHNOLOGY

We have reached the stage where the future development of computer technology has reached its third critical processing juncture. Several choices of direction confront the industry. One direction leads toward giving computers the intelligence to know what they are processing. Another is to apply technology to let people synthesise and create, store and retrieve meaningful pages.

In most circles, one direction is being pursued at the expense of the other. That is dramatically out of step with the times. At CAP International we believe that computer technology must first learn to deal with images properly before it becomes intelligent. The software created around that processing ability will do far more to make computers appear intelligent and to make them easier to handle, than providing computers with an understanding of semantics. Already workers are beginning to depend on pointing devices, icon-based interfaces and manipulation of information in the form of combined text and graphics. Taking advantage of the already established trends in working with compound documents (i.e. pictures, graphs and text combined) is the next big step forward in technology.

The productivity of more and more workers depends on maintaining that momentum; and the world of imaging products is coming to meet that need. Scanners, fax machines, digital copiers, laser printers, colour inkjet printers, digital photography–these are just some of the electronic imaging technologies, which are making their mark in the business environment today. Electronic imaging is more than just a change in technologies used in business. It is a convergence of product categories and with that convergence comes a fundamental, revolutionary change: a shift from words and numbers to images as the basic unit of business communication. This is the third wave of information processing.

ADVANCES IN ELECTRONIC IMAGING

Until recently, the high costs of document creation and storage, printing and production have restricted the application of traditional graphic arts in business. Their use has been confined to mass-produced critical documents, sent out from the company to customers, prospects and the general public.

Advances in electronic imaging technology are bringing, and in many cases have already brought, much of that capability to the desktop. In doing so, it has already contributed to redefining the dimensions of work-flow productivity and

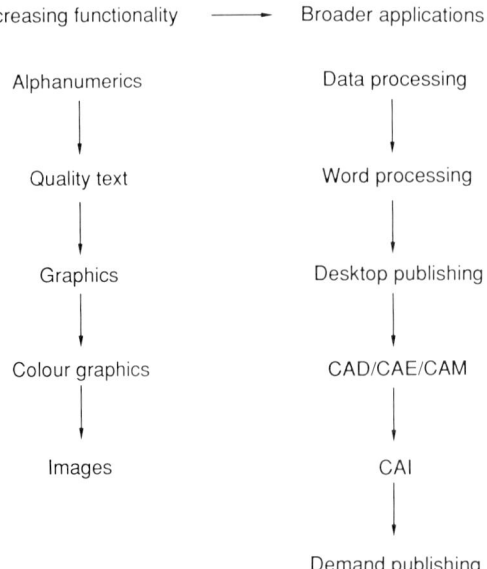

Figure 10.3 Electronic printing

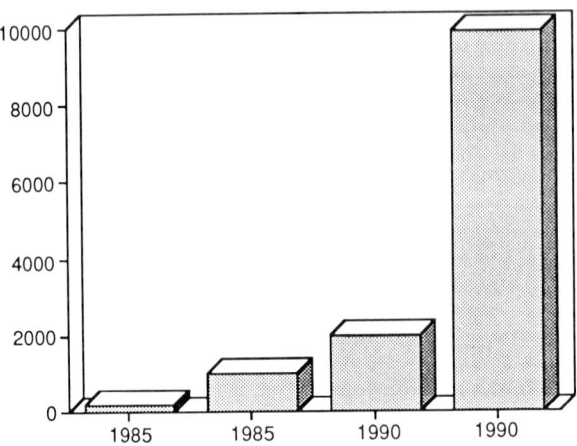

Figure 10.4 Intelligent copier/printer unit placements (US)
(*000's units, 000's dollars*)

this in turn is creating opportunities for technology vendors. Now that the page image can be designed, it needs to be stored on disk, in a data base, transmitted and processed in many other ways. (See Figure 10.3).

Recent developments are providing easy-to-use technology at prices that allow companies to apply concepts from graphic arts to many business communications. The technology itself is creating a tremendous demand within business to communicate in pages that combine text, graphics and

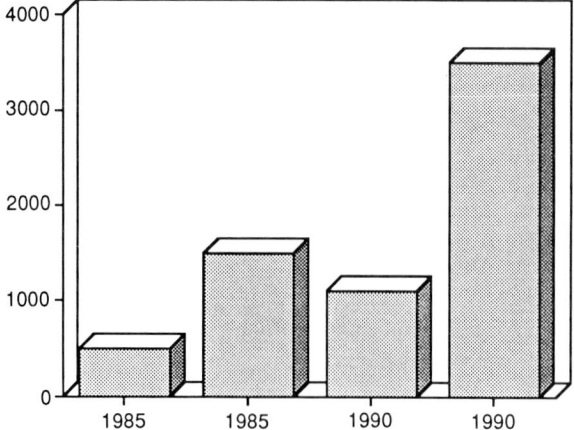

Figure 10.5   Colour hard copy unit placements (US)
(*000*'s *units, 000*'s *dollars*)

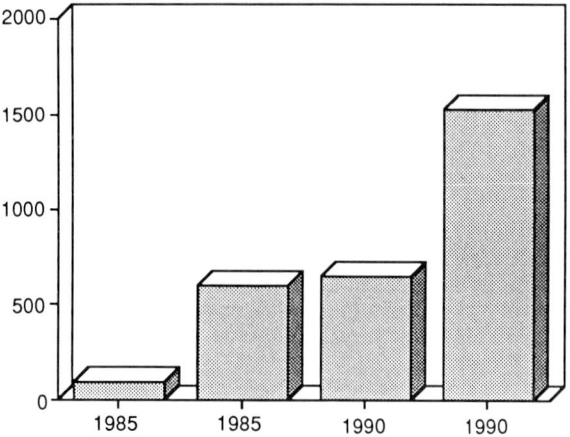

Figure 10.6   Facsimile unit placements (US)
(*000*'s *units, 000*'s *dollars*)

images (see Figure 10.4). The image revolution has arrived quietly through the back door. While printing is only one part of the electronic imaging revolution, it certainly is the major contributor toward the the development of other related technologies and applications. Non-impact printers bring with them the ability to reproduce whatever is displayed on the screen, combining text, graphics and bitmapped images on paper output. They are multi-functional devices, acting as printer and copier simultaneously (see Figure 10.5).

Colour displays are already widely used. Colour output devices, ranging from plotters and inkjet printers to photographic processes, are making their mark as desirable peripherals.

Entire images can be inexpensively transmitted to remote locations and reproduced in hard copy or sent directly to a personal computer by facsimile. Scanners provide the computer with the ability to absorb entire images and store or process them (see Figure 10.6).

Optical disk technology can economically store large quantities of images as images, not supply as characters. Systems capable of storing and retrieving full colour images are increasing in popularity and have myriad applications.

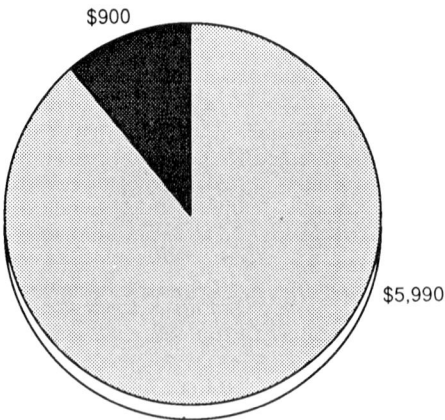

Figure 10.7   Computer publishing systems market–dollar value 1985–1991

The key elements of electronic imaging lie in applying computer technology so that it can communicate ideas, information and knowledge in the same manner as the paper-based processes of storage and dissemination. The challenge to vendors lies not in developing new products but in creating an environment, which can use the convergence of copiers, facsimile, printers and other new technologies.

COMPUTER PUBLISHING – THE FIRST MAJOR APPLICATION

Computer publishing is an example of an immediate environment which can use all of these technologies and set the stage for expanding them. The arrival of desktop publishing within the last two years will contribute even more significantly by transforming individual productivity in a wide range of industries.

Computer publishing involves the electronic capture, creation, editing, layout, composition, presentation and pagination of high-quality text and graphics for documents. Its applications range from newsletters and price lists to sets of technical documentation.

For several years very large businesses have invested in in-house typesetting and printing equipment to produce typeset quality output. This helped them to improve their turnaround times. However, page make-up and insertion of artwork (graphics, photographs, and so on) remains a labour-intensive manual cut-and-paste process. The initial investment is high and the added costs of training and staffing in-house publications departments limit the advantages of traditional in-house publishing over outside commercial services. Those limitations began to disappear in 1983 when turnkey, dedicated computer publishing systems from Interleaf, Texet, Xyvision and others began to enter the market. These new systems responded to the existing needs of business by reducing the cost of producing graphic-arts quality documents. At the same time, they fostered interest in upgrading typewriter-style documents to high quality text and graphics.

Computer publishing systems are central to the electronic imaging revolution. This is where text, illustration and design come together to form page images. Computer publishing systems allow businesses to treat pages as images on at least three levels:

1   They can combine text and many different kinds of picture into documents, including photographs, line drawings and business graphics.

2   Applying graphic design principles does more than make documents look pretty. Proper design helps organise information visually for easy comprehension and retention. Well-designed page layouts, changes in vertical spacing, indents and highlighting of key sections with boxes and separating bars, all help readers find and absorb information. Effective presentation can treble peoples absorption and retention of information.

3   Typography both improves legibility and comprehension and conveys a feeling about the message and the company. Corporate typefaces need to be selected with care because the 'feel' of the typography is a key part of corporate image.

Although expensive dedicated computer publishing systems were the seeds of electronic imaging, desktop publishing – the production of typographic-quality and near typographic-quality page images on desktop computers – is responsible for the recent explosion of interest in communication using images as well as words.

INTEGRATING THE AVAILABLE TECHNOLOGIES

Computer publishing is a milestone towards the developing market for electronic imaging products. It is an environment which combines the current plethora of products, from scanners, facsimile and laser printers to colour image processing and image communications. Already much of that technology has transformed the working environment by emphasising the page image as the standard means of communication.

It has also achieved another breakthrough by bringing electronic imaging into the mainstream of the data processing world. The impact of the widespread adoption of electronic imaging devices has not gone unnoticed by the data processing community; IBM, with the AS 400 and Image Plus extensions has let its direction be known; Wang with its WIIS (Wang Integrated Image System) was the first to point the way and DEC certainly does not intend to be last and is actively pursuing changes in architecture to pursue this market opportunity.

Facsimile, copiers, printers and scanners which replaced telephones, carbon paper and typewriters, are no longer isolated departmental peripherals. Their functions are being combined and integrated into information processing systems.

The first level of integration has already begun, in the form of IC/Ps (intelligent copier/printers). IC/Ps are integrated multi-functional printing systems, which convert information from electronic form into paper-based hard copy. The popularity of these devices in the office cluster and workstation environment will account for 77 per cent of the total IC/P market revenue by 1991. The installed base will grow from 900 000 units in 1987 to 2.1 million units by 1989. Along the IC/P technology path lie numerous possibilities for reversing the information conversion process from paper, back to electronic form.

Facsimile installations have a compound annual growth rate of 35 per cent per year. At that rate they are destined to become the paper-based, person-to-person equivalent of corporate data communication systems. Indeed the link between facsimile and computer is far closer than people often think, new standards in fax communications will pave the way for widespread adoption of fax boards. First extensions to V32 to ensure fax modem compatibility; and second, the advent of ISDN will certainly popularise image communications. Employees can now use hard-copy images as input to computer systems at their workstations, in the form of both digital scanners and fax boards. The potential gains in productivity are high and are typical of the third wave of information processing.

To make best use of this technology, databases will have to be able to deal with images; data communications standards to transmit those images; optical storage systems to store them for later processing and record-keeping. All this may well bring about growth in other areas such as image databases, image networks and image communications.

The integration of all these technologies into a networked image processing system provides electronic imaging industries with big product opportunities. These lie less in vertical specialised market segments than in the world of information processing.

BRINGING ELECTRONIC IMAGING INTO THE MAINSTREAM

So what will the impact of these computer technologies be on the paper-based information distribution process? While keeping information in purely electronic form is clearly still desirable for some industries, the distribution of that information and the preferred way of handling it by individuals will remain paper-based. The quality of the page image, whether produced by an individual, a department or a corporation, will improve dramatically. The convergence of electronic imaging devices will create other environments, which will allow technology migration from high priority applications to low. Image processing requirements will continue to be defined at ever higher levels at the top end of the market and innovation will spread down towards the individual user.

Image processing will thus move from the fringe applications of computer publishing into the mainstream of information processing. Then the third wave will have become visible to all.

Electronic imaging is the critical component of the third wave of information processing. For business, the advances in imaging represent more than tactical gains. For many companies these trends represent a significant strategic potential for managing information. On Wall Street, a major investment firm has integrated a worldwide document communications network into its existing data communications facilities. Not only has the convenience and the user interface (buttons on faxes are very similar to copiers) for sending documents around the world been much improved, but it has looped off some $4 million from its annual telephone bill through using private data lines.

Using imaging computer systems has given some small insurance companies a major edge in competition over larger competitors. By electroncially scanning and processing applications they have reduced the 30-day average processing time for an application to ten days.

Imaging products are no longer merely office commodities. A copier is no longer simply a copier, where the choice of machine depends on how many copies each department needs. Managers need to take into account a new set of capabilities. The digital copier/facsimile, for example, combines output and communications, copying and distributing business correspondence electroni- cally with the same device. Suddenly, a very routine office procedure, the duplication of a document, has become a business communication which is both very difficult to manage and of vital strategic concern.

MANAGEMENT IMPLICATIONS

Most managers understand something about the technology employed by their firm, but now also need to develop an intuition about information technologies, which are on the horizon. They cannot afford to overlook the shift of imaging products from being commodities, handling output, duplication and communication to being a strategic asset in information processing.

In the world of technology there is no boredom, only anxiety or excitement. All live by the same rule: if you do not move quickly to fill a need, someone else will.

11

INFORMATION SYSTEMS IN THE HOME

'The development of the 'electronic cottage' will not be a simple or smooth process. While there will be a wide variety of new applications for computing and communications systems within the home, they will tend to stay as a separate systems for the foreseeable future. These systems will be built around four major applications clusters,' says Garf Collins, Managing Director of BIS Applied Systems.

A POSSIBLE SCENARIO FOR 2020

Alex is at home sitting in the communications lounge. She stares fixedly at the block diagram of a customer's computer on the large wall screen, glancing occasionally at the remotely accessed diagnostic information. She tells the system to access more detailed diagnostics, which reinforces her suspicions about the cause of the fault. On a portion of the screen she checks her company's spares inventory and orders a delivery, printing out installation diagrams and instructions from the service data bank. The telephone chimes and Alex commands the call to start. Hearing her husband Thomas's voice, she keys a command to see his face in a small window of the screen. '. . . not home till 8.oo p.m. tonight. By the way have you organised the carpet man?' She snaps 'command full screen' and examines his features minutedly for traces of insincerity, 'O.K. Thomas, but why do you always think because I work from home, I own all its problems. But don't worry, I'll fix it'.

Alex calls up the carpet company, and talks to the carpet layer. She stores his image for later security use, gives him a password and arranges for him to lay the carpet that afternoon. On impulse she gets him to show a video shot of the carpet, so she can make sure of the shade. Because she would not be in when he calls she defines to the security system the area of the house the carpet man can get into when he gives the password. 'Luckily we have a porch video camera so, from the office, I can check his face with the stored image before letting him in. What did people do in the old days' she mused.

She then just had time to order a gourmet-delivered meal for 9.00 p.m. and to arrange a film. The on-demand films were all recent, so she ordered one to be accessed from the archive collection and to be available for viewing at 10.00 p.m. That night they sat together watching 'Brief Encounter'.

'How odd the small black and white image looks,' thought Alex, as she wiped away a tear. 'Title sums up our life though.' She quietly tapped commands into a key pad. 'Lock external doors, set alarm, close curtains in bedroom, switch on lights – low level, play romantic music'. 'At least we have tonight,' she thought.

MALFUNCTION, MALFUNCTION . . . the words flashed up on a corner of the screen followed by a realistic voice saying 'Bed 1 curtains will not close, lights on will not dim. Repeat. . . .'

The scene above is fiction only in that it could not happen today. Within 30 years our homes may well have fully integrated control, entertainment, computing and communications systems. But the route to this outcome is scattered with economic, cultural and commercial obstacles. This short paper sets out the most likely scenario for the next 15 years with some confidence and for the subsequent 15 with some trepidation. For brevity we will call them period one and period two.

WHAT DRIVES THE 'ELECTRONIC COTTAGE'?

Table 11.1 Basic drivers

☐Genetic	Voice/vision/touch
☐Cultural	Group behaviour
	Low bother threshold
	Pleasure seeking
☐Economic	Wealthy middle-aged

Technology alone cannot drive development in home electronics. The preconditions for acceptance of any new technology lie in basic genetic, cultural and economic factors. The genetic influences go back at least five million years to the time when we diverged from the chimpanzee, a species that has a strong social grouping instinct. We have retained that instinct and added a refined speech process, which seems by now to be inherent. We are genetically predisposed to acting in groups. We perceive the members of the group with all senses and communicate verbally with them. On the other hand we have no genetic predisposition to using keyboards and other temporary technological tools. Because we are so used to processing wide band-widths of information which give presence through vision, hearing and touch, we are intolerant of newer systems, which add complication and remoteness. This genetic background makes us more attracted to watching videos which uses vision and hearing rather than reading from screens or, regrettably, even from books. Except for afficionados we have a low 'bother threshold'. In the home we will not spend time on elegance of information solutions. Rather, we will take the route of least bother to meet our needs.

Economically, period one will be driven by the home needs of the middle-aged affluent. This will continue into period two but retirers will have an increasing influence. These demographic influences will be far stronger than influences based on social need, because the commercial impetus will be towards satisfying affluent or discretionary entertainment expenditure general-ly. There will be a lag before the technology is adapted to meet wider social needs.

Table 11.2 shows the penetration for some technologically based systems. Note that even a simple system like television with very advantageous cost reductions arising from volume took 10 years to penetrate fully. Complex systems usually meet resistance, for example, modular unit audio faltered because the majority of consumers would not worry about interconnection. When the mass market developed it was for ready to plug-in, packaged systems. In the same way, the potentially much more complex home electronics systems of the future will not be fully interlinkable, but will emerge as discrete packages.

Table 11.2   Penetration of technology

	5%	13%	60%	75%
TV	1950			1960
Phone	1950			1983
Car		1950	1983	
Central heating	1960			1985

10 years in ideal case! Much longer if infrastructure cost or bother high

WHAT APPLICATIONS WILL THERE BE?

Given our genetic, social and economic background, we can classify home applications on a pleasure to pain spectrum, broadly as shown in Table 11.3.

The classification from pleasure to pain will obviously vary with the individual. People will regard some applications such as security, as an evil necessity. Their interests in other technological applications will tend to be in direct correlation to the amount of pleasure they bring.

For example, although working at home is associated in some views with pleasure in that it cuts out inconveniences such as commuting, it goes against the genetic and social grain to a significant extent. It is unlikely that in the first period more than ten per cent of individuals will work substantially at home. (At home, of course, is not the same as *from* home—many self-employed people

Table 11.3 What will we do with it?

Use	Example
Entertainment ⎫ News ⎭	Films, shows, music
Social dialogue	Talking, writing
Educational	Study, hobby, home maintenance
Simple transactions	Ordering from catalogue
Picture transactions	Selection of style goods
Work	Linked to office, self-employed
Control/persons	Exercise, medical monitoring
Control/house	Security, device control, metering

Pleasure to pain spectrum determines interest in technology solution

have offices at home but their work takes them elsewhere). The social barrier is strong–most people regard getting out of the home to work as an important part of their social lives. Another problem is that companies find it difficult to maintain identity when people are widely scattered. The pace of the technology is a barrier, here, too. Only in the second period will public telephone systems generally allow companies to give the appearance of a coherent workforce wherever it is scattered.

HOW THE ELECTRONIC COTTAGE WILL EMERGE

Home systems will not evolve as integrated systems, because there will not be a core integration need to attract major suppliers. Instead there will be four clusters of devices serving different driving needs–each of which continues an established tradition of technology use in the home. These will be:

- entertainment cluster
- telecommunications cluster
- control cluster
- computing cluster

The majority of expenditure will be on the entertainments and communications clusters. They will provide the basis for the extension of function within these clusters. The computing and control clusters will be well behind in weight of consumer expenditure, but within the control cluster there will be important niche applications, such as security.

Although these clusters will provide overlapping functions to some extent they will remain fairly distinct, with *ad hoc* interconnections. No wide-spread home Local Area Network (LAN) will emerge to interlink them. During period one, the communication links will be telephone lines, cable and satellite and

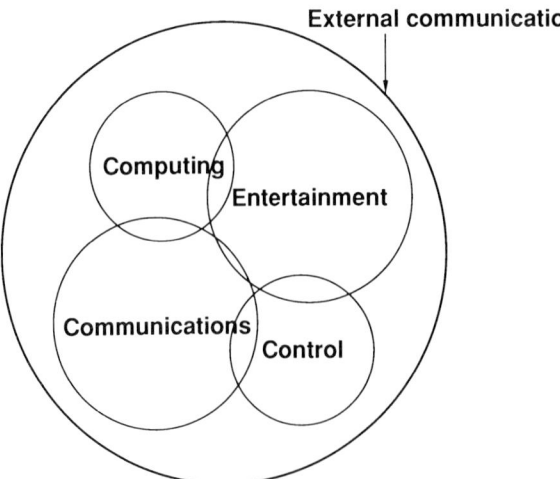

Figure 11.1   Clusters. Size of cluster based on degree of interest, base of existing product and current practice

their derivatives. They will only merge in limited areas as wide-band ISDN becomes available domestically in some areas during the second period.

THE ENTERTAINMENT CLUSTER

Continuing high expenditure on entertainment particularly television will drive the provision of entertainment applications. Television and VCR are examples of very rapid market penetration. Their smooth progression to high levels of market penetration have occurred because they are easy to use. In contrast the home computer grew rapidly, until customers realised there was a high bother content.

Period one

Right now this cluster consists of television, video, separate audio systems, some games-oriented computers, some video cameras and moderate cable and satellite TV reception.

By the end of this period as illustrated in Table 11.4, high definition television and hi-fi sound will be combined. Some homes will have communication links by cable and satellite input to main systems and cable splitting to subsidiary systems. Some houses will also have links to Prestel derivatives for low band-width applications and digital video replay (with CD ROM paramount) for prerecorded media, although VCR will still be significant. Digital communications will begin to provide films on demand.

Table 11.4 Entertainment cluster

High definition TV, hi-fi, audio
Communication links to: Satellite receive only
                         Cable some interaction
                         Broadcast ⎫
                         Telephone ⎬
                         Optical fibre ⎭   small number of households
Video cassette recorder
Video disk (CD-ROM)
Fun computer

Devices as at 2004

The main difference in information content in the home at the end of the period will come from a large digital publishing industry and from retail activities made possible by distribution of high quality recorded images. These will influence many of the basic domestic applications, including entertainment, but they will be particularly important for educational and domestic broad band-width transactions.

End of period two

By this time 80 per cent of homes will have High-Definition TV (HDTV), typically with cable and satellite links as input. Some homes will have interactive on demand television. CD ROM and video interactive transaction systems will be used widely for shopping and education. The beginnings of 3D holography will be provided with locally driven colour television systems.

The high capacity for delivering entertainment will put pressure on quality during the first period. That, in turn will provide an opportunity for more educational and interactive applications to emerge particularly in period two.

THE COMMUNICATIONS CLUSTER

The communications cluster involves two key elements—the underlying communications technology and the device cluster, which centres around the main telephone point(s) in the house. The underlying commmunications development covers a continuous spectrum over the 30 years. Because of the long investment cycles involved there will be some homes still after 30 years with communications services as they are now—the telephone carriers simply can't provide every home with the new technology rapidly enough. Other homes will be dramatically different. Very wide band-width systems will deliver them integrated communications of all kinds.

Period one: underlying communications

In the initial years we will continue with normal telephone communications, progressively adding more lines to each home. Better quality STD and lines and improved modem/codec technology will make it possible to transmit realiably at 20 000 bits per second. The beginnings of ISDN will give unified communications across the whole audio-video spectrum and will make it possible to divide the band-width according to the particular home's applications. This will become increasingly significant as the laying of optical fibre progresses over the period. The cost of installation will remain at a few hundred pounds per urban location. New estates and towns with good cable duct access will be the first to receive optical fibres and the band-width may be rented to service companies to provide, for example, interactive video.

Period two: underlying communications

In this period the pressure for new powers for PTTs and the legal battles fought in period one will begin to have an effect. PTTs will emerge as providers of content as well as carriers. Together with the video firms, they will use entertainment applications to drive the provision of ISDN domestically. Cable will diminish as a medium, giving way to ISDN and satellite broadcasting for fixed programme material. Broadcast telephoning will continue to improve and proliferate. At the beginning of the period satisfactory service for business community mobile telephones will be achieved as sufficient band-width becomes available.

Techniques of separation and new frequencies will gradually make it possible for mobile telephones to work with many more stations and provide the service in the home too. This will become the most common basis for transferring business calls to individuals working at home, because the penetration of ISDN will not be complete anywhere domestically even at the end of the period.

Period one: communications device cluster

There will be proliferation of telephone orientated gadgets such as answering machines, facsimile devices, simple transaction terminals like Minitel, and mobile telephones that provide the equivalent of logical addressing. Simple transaction terminals will be distributed to the point of use anywhere in the house, as a result of an improved standard telephone connection system introduced by PTTs. It really begins to look like a cluster with the increase of the numbers of exchange lines in the house, through a simple switching system. The beginning of video phones will also have an impact. These will initially

Table 11.5 Communications device cluster

Many gadgets	e.g. answering machines
Video phones (few)	slow motion–STD
	full motion–optical fibre
Multiple line control	home switchboard
Simple transaction terminals	as French Minitel
No links with entertainment cluster	fulcrum assumption is optical
	fibre and video phone

Devices as at 2004

provide slow motion TV images but full motion TV will rapidly appear where optical fibre has penetrated. In turn advances in television technology will drive the provision of ISDN/optical fibre. The telephone cluster will not link with the entertainment cluster but will retain its own separate screen. Together with the associated embedded computer these screens will provide terminals capable of carrying out simple transactions. By the end of period one the household will have devices as summarised in Table 11.5.

Period two: communications device cluster

The spectrum at this stage will range from homes still using current (1989) technology to homes at the extreme of innovation. Video phones will become more important as the quality increases and the price drops, with perhaps 30 per cent of homes having one by the end of the period. Optical fibre connections will be widespread, and will facilitate the extension of applications in the entertainment cluster, but the telecoms cluster will not grow to provide general entertainment. Many low band-width directory and transaction services will become available on the special purpose terminal associated with the communications cluster. Customers will use voice input and natural voice synthesis to communicate with them. Video telephone screens will speed up the growth of interactive applications, which involve demonstration from a restricted range of options, for example, initial selection in buying a new car or a wedding dress.

THE COMPUTING CLUSTER

It is important here to distinguish between fun computing (where games and simple computer assisted learning programs will continue to be provided by a small computer as part of the entertainment cluster) and the business applications that will be run on a separate cluster.

The main computing cluster will continue to follow a step behind personal computing technology in businesses. Entrepreneurs such as Alan Sugar of Amstrad will bring the new technology to a much wider market at lower prices.

Period one

The typical business configuration emerging currently is a powerful 16-bit computer with hard disk, low speed modem and links to either special purpose business networks or public systems such as Viewdata and Electronic Mail. Users often dump their disks to a VCR. A separate fax device will increasingly double as a printer.

Well before the end of period one the computers will be 32-bit with very substantial storage of all forms, including re-usable image storage based on optical disks. High quality fax and printing will be combined on the same device. Facilities such as autodialling of telephone numbers from the computer will be commonplace and homes will have two to three telephone lines through a small exchange, which will also provide a service to other household extensions. Basic communication services will be supplemented for home business by the appearance of many electronic document exchange networks for particular industries such as insurance, international trade, financial transactions, as well as more general improved business intercommunications services, which provide translation between incompatible equipment. Towards the end of the period, voice applications will be well developed–voice command will be common and limited vocabularly, continuous speech and voice dictation will begin to have a significant place.

Period two

After the turn of the century the computing cluster will begin to become much simpler from the user's view-point, because it is linked into the ISDN network. As a result, all forms of communication, such as text, voice and facsimile will be available within a single integrated system. Video phone, however, will not typically be linked in with computing cluster directly. Numerous homes will use voice input, for dictating correspondence and for command purposes.

THE CONTROL CLUSTER

The control cluster embraces a number of niche applications, which have some potential interconnection but will initially grow separately.

Period one

At this stage there will be a very strong growth in security systems, with intrusion and disaster sensing equipment linked to a special purpose computer. External surveillance links will increase and most will continue to be turn-key applications, where the householder buys a complete installed system. At the same time, distributed control applications, such as heat and light switching, will begin to be gathered together under control of a single unit, which enables them to be switched on and off remotely. However, because this embraces the products of numerous suppliers it has too much bother content for most households. It is therefore unlikely to be a major growth area in the period.

Period two

Wealthy homes will install increasingly sophisticated security systems with remote video surveillance. Security systems will begin to take over some functions of home control. By the end of the period they will offer householders a wide range of options on a turn-key basis. There will be very little interaction with the other clusters, since the effort to understand interconnections and co-ordinate suppliers will be beyond most householders' aptitude or inclination.

BRINGING IT ALL TOGETHER

How rapidly each of these clusters expands depends on the speed at which improved communications facilities become available. The telecommunications cluster will be most dependent on the facilities at the beginning, followed by the computing cluster, the control cluster and the entertainment cluster. However, entertainment will move to top place rapidly. The biggest imponderable is the extent of the need, which will pull ISDN/optical fibre into the household. The video phone and interactive access to television programme material are the most likely users that will create consumer demand for high band-width communications. This pull should become substantial in the second period. However, if the video shop habit is too entrenched and if people become embarrassed telling white lies over video phones those applications may be slowed down. In that case, business application itself will not be a sufficient driving force. It is probable that all four clusters will all be linked to ISDN by the end of the 30-year period in some homes. However, there will not be substantial systematic linking, or even sharing of facilities, between the clusters, except where the householder has a particular hobby interest in making it happen.

In short, the electronic cottage will occur, but the routes to it will depend upon how the technology clusters develop. Looking ahead as far as we can with confidence, Table 11.6 gives a picture of the kind of applications and technology clusters we can expect to see in the year 2004. Beyond that there

Table 11.6 Uses of technology clusters in 2004

Use		Entertainment	Computer	Communications	Control
			Technology cluster		
Entertainment/news	10	A	C	C	
Social	6		C	A	
Educational	4	A	B		
Simple transactions	3	A	C		
Picture transactions	2	A		C	
Work	2		A	B	
Control/personal	3		B		A
Control/house	2		C		A

Annual spend on use as relative number. Importance of cluster as vehicle as letter. 10 and A most significant

may be a whole new variety of applications and perhaps new technology clusters currently undreamt of. Whatever emerges we can be sure that exploitation of electronic and communications systems within the home has only just begun.

Note: The source material from which the above was synthesised was wide but particular thanks are due to colleagues at BIS Mackintosh for access to their publication 'The Interactive Home'.

POSTSCRIPT:
INFORMATION TECHNOLOGY
THE NEED FOR SKILLS

'The shortage of skilled employees for the IT sector will become increasingly acute in the coming decade, unless companies take remedial action now', argues Richard Pearson, Deputy Director, Institute for Manpower Studies.

Information technology is one of the key ingredients of economic success for both companies and nations. Yet the skills to develop and apply it are in short supply throughout the western world. This chapter looks at the growing demand for IT skills in the context of the UK labour market. It also considers the supply of such people and the actions needed to ensure that their supply is adequate to meet Britain's needs to the end of the century.

Change has been a feature of the labour market since time immemorial. The skills of agriculture and hunting were followed by those of building and the crafts. Agriculture, however, remained the dominant employer until the last century, when both technology and the agricultural revolution began to have a major impact. As a result, while the population of Britain was quadrupling in a century, the numbers working in agriculture slumped from a peak of 2 million in 1850 to 0.3 million today.

The next phase was the rise and fall of manufacturing employment, which rose fivefold to a peak of 12 million in the 1960s, before falling back to today's figure of 6.5 million. We are now well into the service age with nearly two-thirds of the work force (15 million) currently employed in services (Figure 12.1). The Information Age is set to follow.

A major component of this growth in services has been in part-time jobs, which now account for one in four of the total. This figure will rise to about one in three by the end of the century. This growth has been of particular benefit to women, who will soon account for half the labour force. The 1980s have also seen significant changes in the way, in which people have been employed. We now find many more people in the 'peripheral' workforce – not only part-timers but temporaries, people in training schemes, and people working for subcontractors to the big companies.

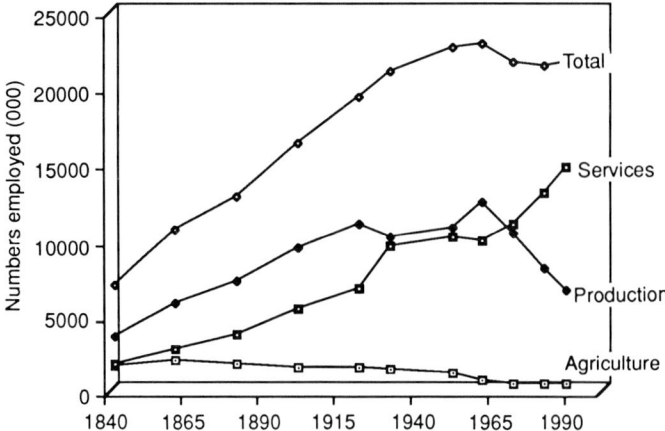

Figure 12.1   Employment in Great Britain 1841–1988 (*Source:* Department of Employment. *Crown copyright. Reproduced by permission of the Controller HMSO*)

The software houses have been among the major beneficiaries of this latter change. This is all part of the process, whereby employers are increasing their flexibility by adjusting manning levels to match base workloads, buying in specialist help on an *ad hoc* basis (Figure 12.2) and training their permanent staff to handle a variety of jobs, rather than specialise in one.

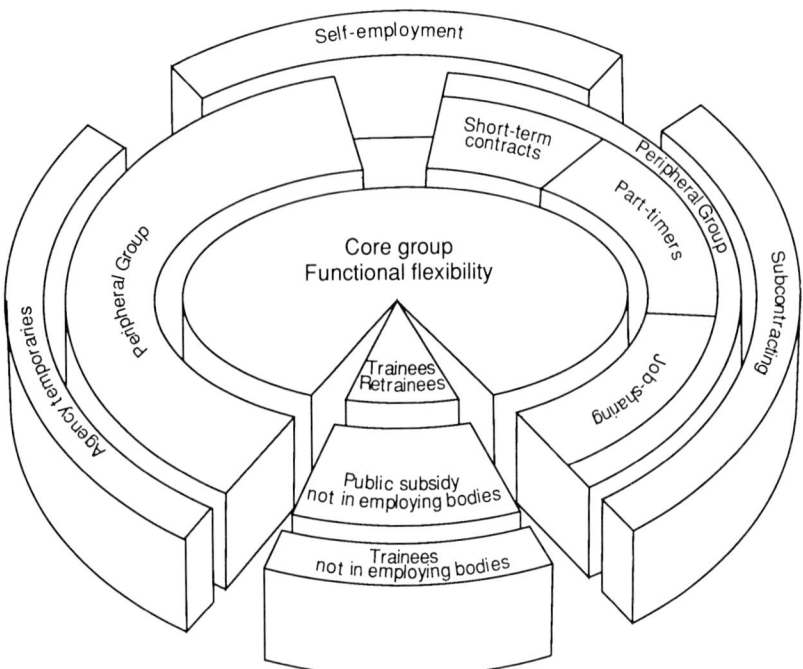

Figure 12.2   The flexible firm

The move towards greater flexibility is supported by the trend towards home working, facilitated by IT. There are more than a million home workers in traditional activities, such as the rag trade and home-based sales. But the growth in home working comes from managers and professionals, particularly in computing, who are working all or part of their time at home, sometimes communicating via the computer and the telecommunications network. While the numbers are small as yet, this is one of the pointers to workstyles in the next century.

Another major change this decade has been the massive rise in unemployment, which peaked in Britain at well over 3 million. Seven years of economic growth has had only limited impact on this figure, giving one of the paradoxes of the UK labour market–the co-existence of high unemployment with growing skill shortages, which now affect one in three firms. An analysis of the unemployed shows them to be largely low-skilled and living in areas of limited job prospects. The most tragic aspect is the one million people who have been unemployed for a year or more. A challenge for the nation is to harness their potential contribution to the labour market (Figure 12.3).

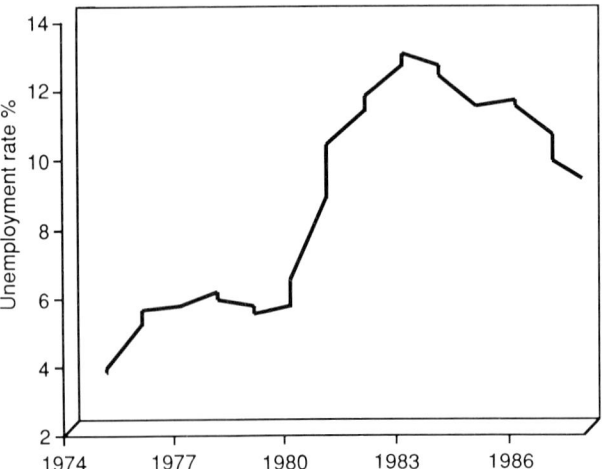

Figure 12.3 Unemployment rate 1975–1988 (*Source:* Department of Employment. Crown copyright. *Reproduced by permission of the Controller HMSO*)

THE INFORMATION TECHNOLOGY SKILLS MARKET

What then does this mean for the IT profession? There are now nearly 250 000 IT professionals in the UK, a total that has been increasing over the last decade at over 5 per cent per year. They represent about one in ten of the professional labour force of the country. In addition, there are several million other professional workers, who are actively involved in using IT, on their desks, in their factories or in their laboratories. The electronics and computer companies are the largest employers of IT professionals outside the government, accounting for about one in three of the total. The largest employs over 10 000. The IT consultancies and software houses employ a further one in five, with the main companies employing more than a thousand each. Among the users, the major employers are in financial and public sectors, with relatively small numbers to be found in the industrial companies (Figure 12.4).

IT staff are generally young and in many cases two-thirds or more are aged under 35; in some software houses the average age is as low as 28. The

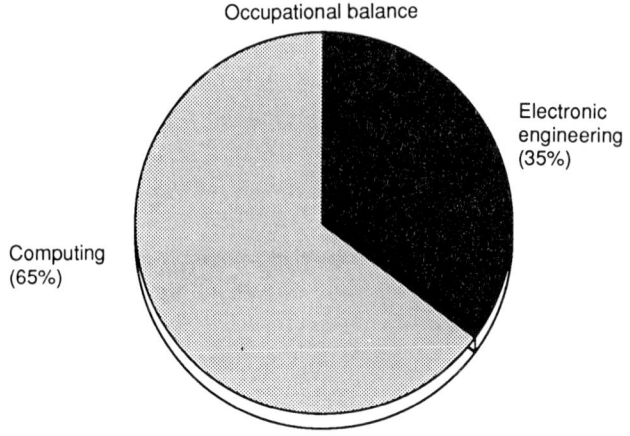

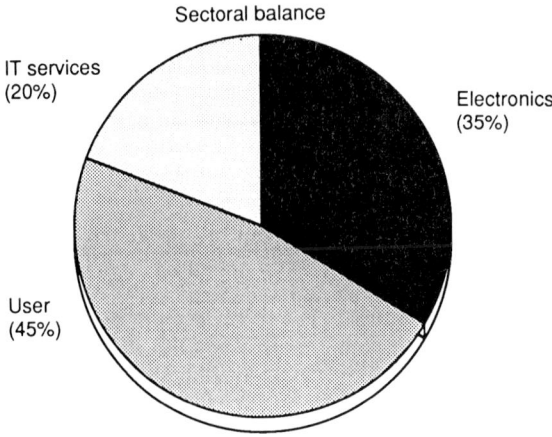

Figure 12.4   IT professionals–1985: occupational balance and sectoral balance. Note: the percentages are approximations. (*Source:* IMS)

profession is also characterised by a low representation of women, well under 10 per cent in the hardware areas and only around 20 per cent in the software areas.

Within IT there are a number of separate occupational groups. The biggest distinction is between those with hardware-based skills, who account for about one in three IT professionals and are mainly employed in the electronics and computer companies; and those with software skills (two out of three), who are employed across all the sectors, but with the biggest concentrations in the software houses and the financial and public sectors.

The end-users, from managers with personal computers, through clerks in banking using a computer database, to sales staff dealing with customers, are now becoming the focus of attention for both suppliers and employers. As a result the traditional data processing function is being tansformed to meet their information and training needs. One solution lies in 'information centres', where IT specialists advise and help the individual user to apply IT. Another involves dispersing IT specialists to work in user departments. Both require IT specialist staff to develop vastly improved interpersonal skills and understanding of the business environment, if they are to be effective. Old-style, central data processing departments are in long-term decline.

Since the mid-1970s there have been continuing shortages of IT skills. In the late 1980s, over half the employers reported major difficulties in recruiting experienced IT staff. Particular shortages arose for people with experience of special applications areas, such as financial systems, or in specialist technological areas, for example networking and artificial intelligence. The main responses by employers to these difficulties continue to be to raise salaries and to invest more in training. Other actions, such as developing links with academic institutions, recruiting less experienced staff and subcontracting more IT work, also feature.

On the salary front, the small electronics firms, the software houses, consultancies and some financial institutions are giving the strongest response; for example, many have introduced quarterly salary reviews to remain competitive. However, many employers, especially the larger ones, are reluctant to raise salaries because of the disruption this causes to internal salary structures and differentials. Moreover, they do not want to bid up the price in a market where the short-term supply is fixed.

Although firms report an increase in training investment, the amount provided is still generally low, especially in the area of continuing training or career development. The main driving force for training remains the individual and his or her line manager. The training function still has a servicing rather than a motivating role in most organisation. Its emphasis is almost exclusively on updating technical skills and it initiates training in a fairly *ad hoc* manner.

While the main source of new entrants to the profession is new graduates, most companies rely heavily on recruiting experienced staff, which simply means reshuffling the existing people within the market. On average, two experienced staff are taken on for each newly-qualified graduate recruited from higher education, a figure that has changed little throughout the 1980s. Approximately 6000 graduates with IT skills and 2000–3000 from other disciplines were being recruited to IT jobs each year in the mid-1980s. The major recruiters are the electronics, computing and software companies. The eight largest recruited over 3000 graduates between them in 1988, accounting for about half the total UK output. Only a minority of organisations (mostly those in the financial and public sectors), retrain or upgrade their own staff to meet their growing needs for IT skills (Figure 12.5).

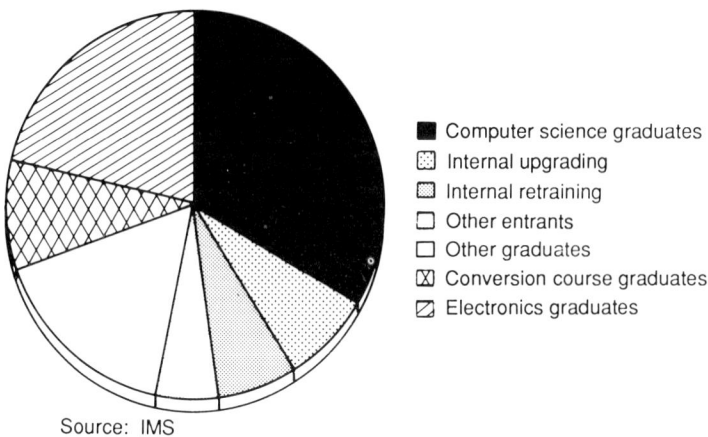

Computer science graduates
Internal upgrading
Internal retraining
Other entrants
Other graduates
Conversion course graduates
Electronics graduates

Source: IMS

Figure 12.5   Entrants ot IT (*Source:* IMS)

Electronic and software engineering graduates are primarily recruited by the electronics and computer companies. Other employers seek only very small numbers. All sectors are recruiting computer science graduates for computing and data processing work. However, there is still considerable debate and divergence of attitude towards computer science degrees. These are still a relatively new discipline in higher education, having only emerged in significant numbers in the 1980s.

On the one hand, the quality of graduates taking these courses has risen significantly. That together with an improvement in the quality of many courses, is making these graduates increasingly attractive. Others, however, see many of the courses as being too theoretical, making people interested in computers *per se*, rather than as tools, and lacking in more practical elements. By contrast, the conversion courses, in which non-IT graduates undertake a one-year postgraduate course to learn IT, have proved a valuable additional recruitment source providing 1000 extra IT graduates each year.

For many computing and data processing jobs the key selection method nevertheless remains the use of an aptitude test–for these graduates are being sought regardless of discipline, with non-IT graduates often accounting for half the intake (Figure 12.5).

Although demand has grown by more than 50 per cent in the decade, it has been sensitive to major national and international market developments. This was graphically illustrated by the events of 1986, when the computer industry worldwide went into recession and the British government cut back the growth in defence spending. As a consequence, several of the major computer and electronics groups slashed their graduate intakes, in one case down from a high of 560 to 60, in another from 140 to 50. In both cases, these figures contrasted with an increase that had been projected the year before. This has adversely affected the recruitment image of the industry.

FUTURE PROSPECTS

The 1980s have seen near-continuous growth in demand for IT staff and two government initiatives have boosted the output of IT graduates, yet the decade ends with continuing skill shortages. What then are the prospects to the end of the century?

Employment in the industry will continue to rise, with half the new jobs that are created in the decade to 1995 being at graduate level and above (Figure 12.6). Unfortunately this will be of only limited benefit to the unemployed, whose total is unlikely to fall significantly for some years. The demand for professional IT staff will continue to grow across the economy, increasing by

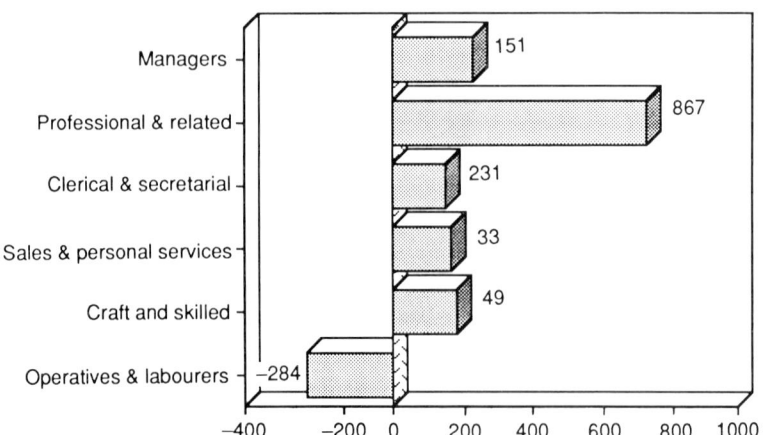

Figure 12.6   Changes in occupational employment 1986–1995 (thousands) (*Source: Review of the Economy and Employment 1987*, Institute for Employment Research, University of Warwick. *Reproduced by permission*)

around 5 per cent per year. This would give a total employment level of over 300 000 in the mid-1990s. This rate of growth, however, depends on both the speed of introduction of IT, the rate of economic growth and the conti..uing flow of inward investment from overseas companies into the UK.

Given the blurring of occupational boundaries and the uncertainty over the precise pattern of growth in demand, any detailed occupational forecasts would have a spurious accuracy. More certain are the changes in the skill balance which will include:

1 the growing importance of software and of systems engineering experience;
2 the blurring of the hardware/software divide;
3 the growing importance of interacting with the customer and user and the need for technical staff to have both applications and commercial skills and improved interpersonal skills;
4 the continuing high demand for project management skills.

The much-promised demise of the programmer, predicted for the last decade, is still many years away. However, the nature of the job is changing, requiring more systems analysis skills, better interpersonal skills and more direct interaction with the user. Whether demand will continue to grow beyond the end of the century, however, is less certain – software productivity will at some stage make a breakthrough with the fifth generation.

On the supply side, a time bomb has been ticking away for the last 20 years. The downturn in the birthrate in the 1960s and 1970s and the consequential massive downturn in the number of school-leavers over the period to 1994 will exacerbate recruitment problems. In 1984 there were nearly a million school-leavers; by 1988 the figure had dropped to nearer 850 000. Over the six-year period to 1994 there will be further plunge to about 600 000 a year (Figure 12.7).

This is going to hit employers in two ways. Firstly, in many areas of the country, there will be serious shortages of school-leavers, especially at the 5 O Level/2 A Level standard. Secondly, it will reduce the flow of entrants into higher education at a time when demand is booming. The net effect is that while the output of higher education will continue to grow to 1992, it will then fall back until 1998 (Figure 12.8).

This all presupposes that more of the age group go to higher education, as do more mature entrants and those with non-traditional academic qualifications. A futher problem affecting IT is the swing by students away from studying engineering and technology subjects. This trend is also apparent in the US. As a result, while the supply of IT graduates is likely to continue to rise until 1992, thereafter it, too, will turn down. These increasingly scarce IT graduates will be sought not only by IT companies but by professions, finance and other areas of commerce.

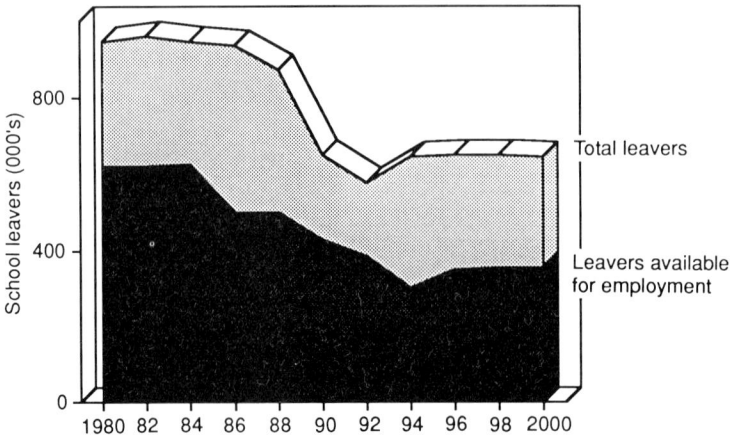

Figure 12.7   Trends and projections of the number of school leavers (*Source:* NEDO based on adjusted data from the Department of Education and Science (England only), Scottish Education Department and Welsh Office.)

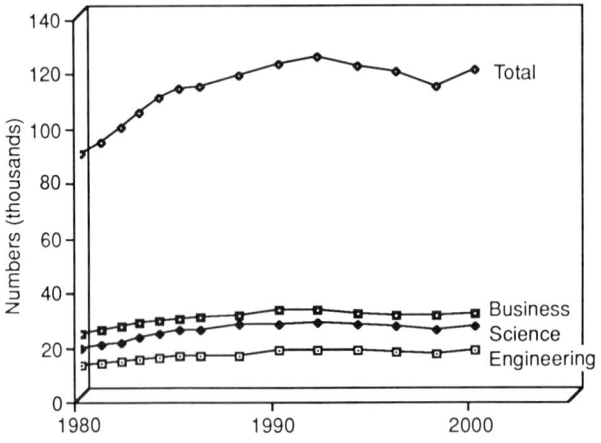

Figure 12.8   First degree graduate output 1986–2000–all sectors (*Source:* IMS)

A PROGRAMME FOR ACTION

What then should be done to ensure a sufficient pool of the skills to develop and apply IT into the next century? Firstly, there is a need for employers to review current recruitment policies, which are often very restrictive in terms of the level and subject of qualification sought. Many recruiters operate with their hands tied behind their backs, for example, restricting recruitment to the universities and ignoring the polytechnic, college and Open University

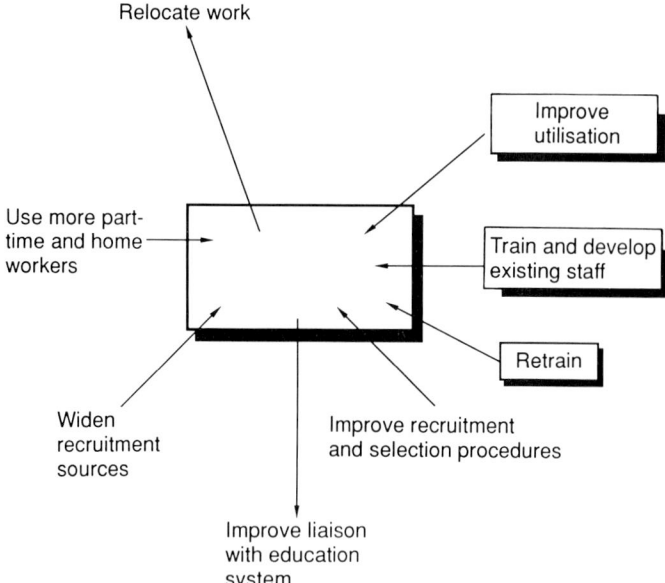

Figure 12.9   Policy options (*Source:* IMS)

graduates. In practice, non-graduates are often just as effective as graduates in many IT jobs.

The financial and government sectors, are regularly retraining and developing internal candidates. Other sectors rarely do so. Mature graduates, who will form a rising proportion of the total, will present challenges to firms in the IT industry, which has a strong youth culture. Employees will increasingly find that improvements in selection and induction can reduce turnover and hence the need to recruit.

Using IT will allow companies to locate more work outside the high pressure South Eastern labour market and to make better use of part-timers and home working. Developing better links with schools and with further and higher education will not only aid recruitment, it will also help boost interest in IT subjects and careers, especially among women, so enlarging the pool of potential recruits in the future.

However, the vast majority of people needed to work in IT at the end of the century are already in jobs. A key need, therefore, is to improve the use of these people and increase their skills, as the potential to use new entrants to the labour force to upgrade a company's workforce in the 1990s will be extremely limited (Figure 12.9).

APPENDIX

BIOGRAPHIES OF THE CONTRIBUTORS

David Clutterbuck is Chairman of the Item Group, a communication project management company. He is editor of the journals: *Strategic Direction, Technology Strategies, Issues* and *Marketing Business.* He is author or co-author of numerous books on mangement themes including *The Winning Streak*

Brian Allison, BSc (Econ)

Brian Allison is an economics graduate who after a Royal Airforce Commission gained his intitial business and marketing experience with Shell-Mex, and BP and Spicers. In 1964, he founded The BIS Group Ltd (of which he is still a Director), and was Executive Chairman of BIS until 1987, when he was promoted to the Board of NYNEX Information Solutions Group, Inc., BIS's parent and a subsidiary of NYNEX Corporation.

Brian Allison is also a Director of English China Clays PLC and Brammer PLC, is a Visiting Professor at the University of Surrey and a member of Economic and Social Research Council. He has lectured extensively on management and marketing for a variety of professional, industrial and commercial organisations.

Alan Bigg, BA (Oxon)
Alan Bigg is the Chairman of Christian Brann
Limited. A graduate in English of Oxford University,
Alan Bigg joined Christian Brann six years ago after
an extensive career in advertising agencies. He held a
senior position in SSC&B:Lintas in London, and ran
his own advertising agency.

While at Christian Brann, Alan Bigg has been
extensively involved with developing strategies for the
introduction of Direct Marketing methods to
companies who had not previously used the
technique. Because of his background in conventional
advertising, he has had a particular mission to develop
ways to intergrate Direct Marketing activity with brand
image development.

Garfield Collins, BSc
Garfield Collins, Managing Director of BIS Applied
Systems graduated in Physics at London University
and worked for some years in electronics research. He
has worked in many industries on projects across the
information services spectrum. Particular professional
interests outside management are information systems
strategy and development method. Garf has published
books on these subjects in Japan, USA, Russia as well
as the UK.

**Frank Gelber, BSc, B Ec(Hons), PhD(Economics,
University of Sydney)**
Dr Frank Gelber has worked for BIS Shrapnel since
August 1981 and was appointed Director and Chief
Economist for BIS Shrapnel in 1984. His main
responsibilities have been in the operation of the
ongoing subscription services involving evaluation of
developments and forecasts of prospects in the
Australian economy (economic outlook, long-term
forecasts) and in the property and building industries
(building industry prospects, building in Australia). He
has also conducted a wide range of industrial and
market research assignments.

In addition to his regular presentations at
conferences and seminars, Frank has given private
briefings on economic prospects for companies as an
aid to the planning budgeting process.

Michael Gordon, MSc, M ENG Sc

Michael graduated from Queen's University, Belfast with a BSc in electrical engineering and an MSc in electronics. He has a M Eng Sc in industrial engineering obtained at the University of New South Wales in Australia.

Michael has worked as an electronics design engineer with GEC, British Aerospace and Amalgamated Wireless Australasia, and as a management consultant, with PA International and Booz Allen. Later, Michael returned to his country of origin to work for the Northern Ireland Development Agency as Executive Director–New Business. He served on the Board of Directors of some eight new companies and became managing director of one of them, American Monitor International.

Michael joined BIS Mackintosh as Managing Director in December 1982 and has recently been appointed Chairman. He was appointed to the BIS Group Board in 1987 as Managing Director of the BIS Marketing Information Group which includes BIS Mackintosh, CAP International in the USA and BIS Shrapnel in Australia.

G M Roger Graham OBE

Roger Graham, OBE, is Chairman and Managing Director of the BIS Group. After graduating from Cambridge and working in the heavy electrical and aircraft industries he entered the computer field in 1961. For five years, he was with IBM both in the United States and the United Kingdom. In May 1969, he became Chief Executive of the computing services activity of the BIS Group.

Roger Graham has been President of the United Kingdom and European Computing Services Associations and was the founding President of the Computing Services Industry Training Council.

Richard Pearson BSc, MSc

Richard Person is currently Deputy Director at the Institute of Manpower Studies, where he has been responsible for the development of the Institute's research programme. His background is in economics and statistical research. He has extensive experience stretching back over the last decade of research and consultancy concerning changing employment patterns and education and training policy, particularly as they affect the highly qualified and the new technologies. He has worked for companies, agencies and government departments in the UK and overseas. He has authored a number of major reports including three major reports abut IT employment, *IT Manpower into the 1990s* (IMS), *The IT Manpower Monitor* (IMS), *Switching on Skills* (NEDO), as well as *UK Occupation and Employment Trends into the 1990s* (Butterworths) which was the report on the UK's largest employer-based forecasting study. He publishes and lectures widely.

Gad J. Selig, PhD

Dr Gad J. Selig is Vice President and General Manager of NYNEX's Complex Systems Integration Group. He is also responsible for marketing, technology and business development for NYNEX Information Solutions Group.

Gad holds a doctorate in International Business, Finance and he has attended advanced management programmes at M.I.T., Columbia University, and the Wharton Business School at the University of Pennsylvania.

He is the author of two books on information management and numerous articles, and has lectured widely both in the US and abroad. He is an adjunct professor of Management and Information Technology and is associated with several universities. Gad is a member of the Society for Information Management and a founder of the Information Technology Roundtable.

Casimir S. Skrzypczak

Casimir Skrzypczak is Vice President of NYNEX's Science and Technology department and is responsible for the formulation of NYNEX's strategic technology plans. Prior to joining NYNEX, Casimir was Vice President of Network Planning at Bell Communications Research Inc.

He has published numerous articles on telecommunications network planning and evolution and is a frequent invited speaker at National and International Telecommunications Conferences. He is a member of Tau Beta Pi and IEEE and has served on a number of National Research Council panels.

Casimir is currently a member of the Board of Directors of the Exchange Carriers Standards Association (ECSA) and chairs its Standards Advisory Committee. He is the founding co-chairman of the Eastern Communications Forum and is currently serving as Technical Program Chairman of ICC '89. He is a Director of the Corporation for Open Systems (COS).

Raimund Wasner

Raimund Wasner is Senior Vice President of new business development at CAP International. A graduate of the University of California at Berkeley, Raimund is now responsible for identifying new business opportunities, researching new technologies, and determining how these technologies can be utilised for maximum efficiency by businesses both domestically and internationally.

Raimund has been involved in the computer and computer software industry for the last 12 years. He spent three and a half years at the Yankee Group as executive director of research and has been involved with a variety of emerging technologies, including the creation of the first hand-held talking translator, and assessing the development of computer technology in the Far East.

Robin Wood B.Com,LLB,Dip IFM

Robin Wood qualified as an advocate of the Supreme Court of South Africa subsequent to majoring in economics and then completing an LLB. After working as a corporate lawyer, he joined Citicorp as an international merchant banker, then joined Trustbank as a Strategic Planner. While at Trustbank he developed and managed TrustLink, an on-line real-time electronic banking system.

He subsequently joined the PA Consulting Group where he specialised in the effective planning of information systems in large organisations.

Robin has been the BIS Group Marketing and Planning Manager since 1988. He is currently reading for a PhD on the key success factors for successful information systems planning in the top 500 British corporations.

INDEX